GRAPH PAPER
From Your
COPIER

W9-ALK-129

John S. Craver

Editor: Bill Fisher; Art Director: Don Burton;
Typography: Joyce Bush, Cindy Coatsworth, Joanne Porter; Photography: Ted DiSante.

Buy this book at your local bookstore or office-supply center or directly from the publisher:

Published by H.P. Books, P.O. Box 5367, Tucson, AZ 85703   602/888-2150
ISBN 0-89586-045-7
Library of Congress Catalog Card 80-80170
© 1980 Fisher Publishing, Inc.
Printed in U.S.A.

How To Copy Graphs

The difference between a page of numbers and a graph is ten minutes of explanation.

A table of numbers is hard to analyze. You can see the large ones, the small ones and whether they increase or decrease, but only a graph can quickly show percentage relationships, trends, seasonal variations, geographic distribution and areas of concentration.

This book contains 204 different graphs of 11 different types and tells you how to use some of them in business and scientific applications, as well as at home and in your artistic endeavors. The data-collection tables are extremely helpful for scheduling. You can copy any of these graphs on your copying machine.

This book explains how to draw and use graphs. Simplified mathematical and statistical explanations are used to explain graph construction.

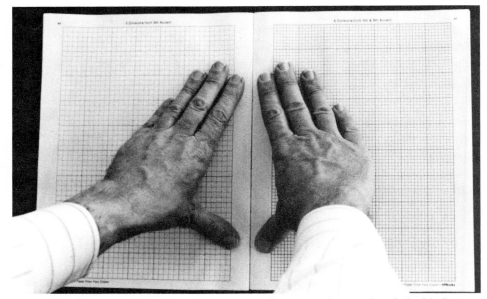

Before copying graphs from the middle of the book, you may have to break the binding so it opens completely.

HOW TO USE THIS BOOK

Most copying machines have a platen or cover which can be raised out of the way to allow copying magazines or books while you hold the pages flat against the copier. To make distortion-free copies, hold the page you want to copy absolutely flat against the glass copy area of your copying machine. This may require "breaking" the binding of this book so the entire page can lay flat against the copy area.

If you can't hold the graph flat enough, or if you want to use the page as your master graph, tear out the page very carefully. Or cut it out with a razor blade or sharp knife, being careful to cut only through the desired page. Replace the page when you have finished so it will be there the next time you need to copy that graph.

If your copier requires inserting individual sheets or pages, you must remove the page as I just described.

HOW TO MAKE MASTERS

First copy the graph, add the title, scales and other necessary markings to the copy. This becomes your *master* graph. Make copies of this master and use them to prepare your graphs. If you make an error in preparing a graph, make additional copies of the master and start over.

While it is easier to copy the graph from the book and use that first-generation copy to create a labelled master to make additional copies, you may prefer to remove the original page from the book, add labels and use it for your master. This will give somewhat darker lines on your copies.

When you are using log-type graphs with very close spacing between some lines, use the book page as the master to provide graph copies with better definition in the fine-line areas.

SAME-SIZE COPIES

Most copying machines produce copies the same size as the original, but some make slightly reduced or enlarged copies. The size change is usually not noticeable and is less than 1/4 of 1% per generation. It is important to know that you may get a reduced or enlarged copy if you are preparing architectural drawings using a scale. You could waste hours plotting measurements with the scale on a grid with dimensions slightly different than you thought they were.

At times it is necessary to copy points from one graph to another by measuring and copying their positions with a pair of dividers. Or, you may place one graph over another on a light table and trace the points. When you do this the grids must be exactly the same size. This can be checked by superimposing one graph over another and holding them up to a strong light to see if the lines match.

Here's a simple test to determine whether your copier makes same-size copies: Make two pencil marks about 10-inches apart on a sheet of plain paper. Copy this sheet. Fold the resulting copy so the marks are at the fold. Marks on the copy should match those on the original if your copier makes same-size copies.

ENLARGED OR REDUCED-SIZE COPIES

Some copying machines offer fixed or variable reduction. When using this type of machine, it is best to create your graphs full-size before making smaller copies. It is much easier to plot points and draw lines on a full-size copy than to work on one which has been reduced.

LACK OF CONTRAST— LIGHT COPIES

The amount of contrast on a copy will vary with both the "exposure control" and the amount of toner in the copying machine. Make sure there is an adequate supply of toner in the copier if you want black lines.

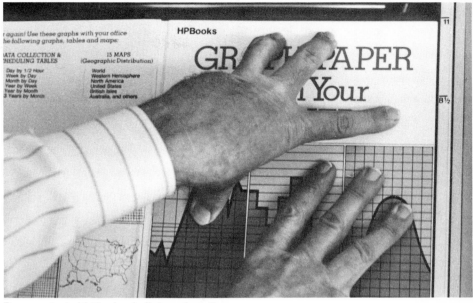

Be sure to hold the book flat against the copier to get a clean copy with minimal distortion.

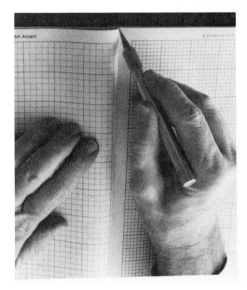

When using a sheet-fed copier, remove the page from the book with a razor knife.

This simple test will illustrate whether the copier you use makes same-size copies.

What Is A Graph?

A graph is a pictorial presentation of numbers made by assigning values to each of a set of horizontal and vertical lines called a *grid*. Marks represent positions of a series of numbers. Graphs can be used to show such things as room temperature, daily changes in stock-market prices and the size and shape of a building. This is not as complicated as it sounds. You use graphs every day.

Graphs can be one-, two-, or three-dimensional, meaning they can show one set of numbers, two sets, or three sets.

One-Dimensional Graphs are used to plot a single set of numbers such as the gallons of gas in your car's tank. The thermostat on your home heating system is another example.

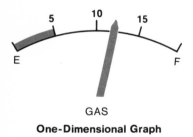

One-Dimensional Graph

Two-Dimensional Graphs are used to plot two sets of numbers. The accompanying graph compares plant growth over a period of time. It could have also related plant growth to amount of light, fertilizer, or water.

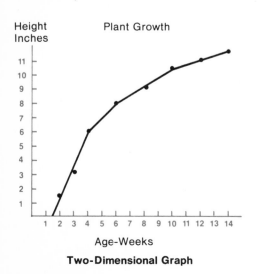

Two-Dimensional Graph

Three-Dimensional Graphs are used to plot three sets of numbers. This graph shows a line formed by an equation with three variables X, Y and Z. The line starts at Point A (X=1, Y=1, Z=3) and ends at Point B (X=3, Y=4, Z=2).

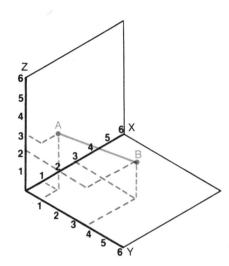

Line between two points (orange)
Point A X = 1 Y = 1 Z = 3 (red)
Point B X = 3 Y = 4 Z = 2 (blue)
Three-Dimensional Graph

X AND Y AXES

In a two-dimensional graph the *horizontal* line is called the *X axis*. The *vertical* line is called the *Y axis*. The point where they cross is called the *zero point*, *point of origin*, or simply *origin*. Values increase on both axes as they move away from the origin.

X axis or horizontal axis is almost always used to plot *time* or the *cause* of an event. In the plant-growth graph the X axis was used to plot time, but it could have been used to plot water or fertilizer. The cause is often called the *independent variable*. It has a fixed sequence of numbers such as hours in a day, grams of water or fertilizer.

Y axis or vertical axis is almost always used to plot the *effect* of that cause, called the *dependent variable*. It is a set of values varying in relationship to the independent variable; for example, temperature at different times of the day.

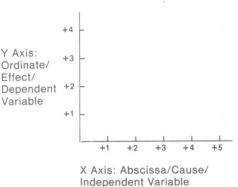

When two variables are dependent on each other, or both depend on some other factor, one variable is arbitrarily placed on the X axis and the other on the Y axis.

The horizontal axis is always numbered with ascending numbers from left to right. A distance along this axis is called the *abscissa*. The vertical axis is always numbered with ascending numbers from bottom to top. A distance along this axis is called the *ordinate*.

DIVISION OR SCALE LINES

If you draw perpendicular lines from the X and Y axes you create a series of squares called a *two-dimensional grid*. These lines are called *divisions* or *scale lines*.

Divisions on an axis must be spaced uniformly in some mathematical progression, but they need not be the same for both. To make graphs easier to read, periodic lines are made bold, or accented.

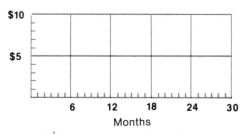

Different scales on X and Y axes.

For example, the X axis may have 12 divisions per major accent to represent months, with the accent lines marking years. The Y axis may have 10 divisions per major accent to represent dollars, with the major accent lines marking $10 intervals.

Or, the X axis may have an arithmetic scale while the Y axis has a logarithmic or geometric scale. *Logarithmic* refers to the spacing between grid lines and is usually abbreviated as *log*. The graph below has an arithmetic scale on the X axis and a logarithmic scale on the Y axis. It is called a *semi-log grid*.

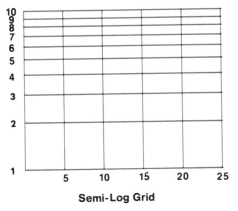

Semi-Log Grid

Scale lines applied to the X, Y and Z axes of a three-dimensional grid look like a series of triangles.

PLOTTING NEGATIVE NUMBERS

Negative numbers (–1, –2, –3, and so forth) can show how far you are below sea level or how much you have overdrawn your bank account. Many phenomena are best illustrated by including negative numbers on a graph.

To show negative numbers, place the origin or zero point in the middle of the paper. Plot negative numbers by extending the X axis to the left, and the Y axis downward. The X or horizontal axis is numbered in ascending negative order from the origin to the left. The Y or vertical axis is numbered in ascending negative order from the origin downward.

Plotting Negative Numbers

In the above graph

```
Point A is in position X =  +1, Y =  +2
Point B is in position X =  +2, Y =  -2
Point C is in position X =  -3, Y =  -3
Point D is in position X =  -2, Y =  +1
```

This list of points shows their location or abscissa by horizontal distance from zero on the X axis. The ordinate or distance from zero is shown on the Y axis. Thus the abscissa of Point D is X = –2, while the ordinate is Y = +1.

The four areas created by the two axes are called *quadrants*.

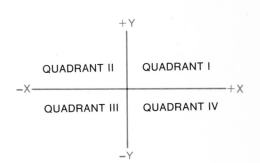

Most graphs deal with *positive* numbers and are plotted in quadrant I. In such graphs the origin or zero point is placed in the lower-left corner. If all four quadrants are used, the origin is placed in the center of the graph.

THREE-DIMENSIONAL GRAPHS

Three-dimensional graphs are used to plot three sets of numbers. Like two-dimensional graphs, the X and Y axes start from the origin. A third line called the *Z axis* starts from the origin and extends vertically at a 90° angle thru the plane formed by the X and Y axes.

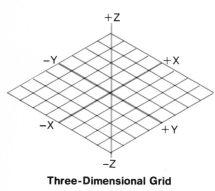

Three-Dimensional Grid

Z Axis is numbered from the origin with positive numbers above the plane and negative numbers below the plane.

Like the scales of a two-dimensional grid, each scale of a three-dimensional grid must follow a mathematical progression. The scales used on each axis may be different.

Isometric Grids are used to draw an isometric projection in which vertical lines are shown as vertical. Both side and top views are at 30° to the horizontal.

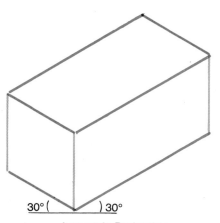

Isometric Projection

Orthographic Grids are used to draw an oblique sketch with front dimensions shown at right angles to each other and the side view at either 30° or 45° to the axis. This is called *orthographic* projection.

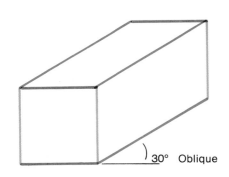

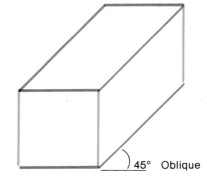

Orthographic Projections

Perspective Grids are used to draw perspective drawings similar to isometric drawings except that front, side and top views are drawn toward a vanishing point rather than at 30° to the horizontal axis.

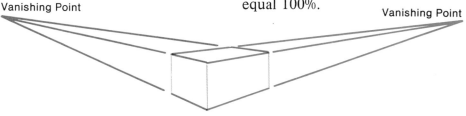

Perspective Drawing

Triangular-Coordinate Grids

are used to draw a graph of three percentage relationships, the total of which equals 100%.

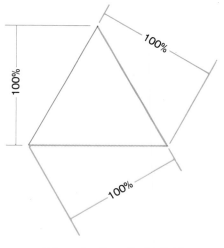

Triangular Coordinate Grid

Each percentage is shown as a line drawn from the center of the base of any side of an equilateral triangle toward its apex. The percentage is represented as the percentage distance from the base toward that apex.

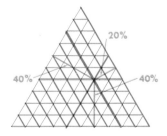

Triangular Coordinate Grid

When lines representing two percentages are drawn, the third percentage can be found by extending the grid lines that cross the tops of the two percentage lines until they meet. The distance of this point from its base, plus the sum of the distance of the other two points from their bases, will equal 100%.

How To Draw a Graph

STEPS IN DRAWING A GRAPH

Drawing a graph is easy if you use these steps:

- Collect Data
- List Data
- Convert Data
- Round Data
- Determine Graduation of Data
- Select Grid
- Scale Grid
- Label Axes
- Title Graph
- Plot Data Points
- Connect Data Points, if desired
- Identify Data Points, as required

Collect the Data—Use uniform time intervals, or, if the dependent variable (X axis) is not time, use uniform-size data sampling so the points you plot will fall on the X-axis division lines.

List Data—Follow a sequence, starting with the smallest value of X so the values can be plotted from left to right. A series of data-analysis tables is provided on pages 33 to 40, for this purpose. Each has columns for the following operations.

X Days	Y Weight		
1	7 oz.		
2	9 oz.		
3	11-1/2 oz.		
4	14 oz.		
5	18-1/4 oz.		
6	1-5/16 lb.		
7	1 lb. 9 oz.		
8	2 lb. 10 oz.		
9	3 lb. 8 oz.		
10	4 lb. 2 oz.		
11			
12			

Example of Data Collection Days are independent variable, or X axis Weight is dependent variable or, Y axis

Convert Data—Use a uniform system of measurement. You can use metric, English, decimal, fractions or whatever you want as long as the data is in the same units.

X. Days	Y Weight	Y Decimal Weight lbs.	
1	7 oz.	0.4375	
2	9 oz.	0.5625	
3	11-1/2 oz.	0.71875	
4	14 oz.	0.875	
5	18-1/4 oz.	1.140625	
6	1-5/16 lb.	1.3125	
7	1 lb. 9 oz.	1.5625	
8	2 lb. 10 oz.	2.625	
9	3 lb. 8 oz.	3.500	
10	4 lb. 2 oz.	4.125	
11			
12			

Data converted to decimal pounds

Round Data—Use the level of accuracy you will need for the graph. For example, round hundredths and thousandths to tenths. Or, round tenths to whole numbers.

X Days	Y Weight	Y Decimal Weight lbs.	Y Weight Rounded 1/10 lbs.
1	7 oz.	0.4375	0.4
2	9 oz.	0.5625	0.6
3	11-1/2 oz.	0.71875	0.7
4	14 oz.	0.875	0.9
5	18-1/4 oz.	1.140625	1.1
6	1-5/16 lb.	1.3125	1.3
7	1 lb. 9 oz.	1.5625	1.6
8	2 lb. 10 oz.	2.625	2.6
9	3 lb. 8 oz.	3.500	3.5
10	4 lb. 2 oz.	4.125	4.1
11			
12			

Decimal data rounded

HOW TO ROUND NUMBERS

There are several ways to round numbers. The most common follows this rule:

1.1 rounds to 1	1.5 rounds to 2
1.2 rounds to 1	1.6 rounds to 2
1.3 rounds to 1	1.7 rounds to 2
1.4 rounds to 1	1.8 rounds to 2
	1.9 rounds to 2

With this rule a number will round *down* four times of the nine and will round *up* five times of the nine, introducing a *statistical bias*.

A preferred rule reduces statistical bias by rounding 0.5 to the next-lower number half of the time and to the next-higher number the rest of the time.

Under this rule, rounding increases an *odd* preceding number when 0.5 is rounded but does *not* increase an *even* preceding number when 0.5 is rounded, thus:

1.5 rounds to 2	3.5 rounds to 4
2.5 rounds to 2	4.5 rounds to 4

Because the preceding number has an equal chance of being odd or even, no statistical bias is introduced. 0.1 through 0.4 still round down to the next lower number and 0.6 through 0.9 are rounded to the next-higher number.

Determine Graduation of Data— Examine the data in your table. Select a graph paper that can cover the range of the data on *both* axes, with major divisions corresponding to the nature of the data.

If the data is in fractions, use paper with the same number of divisions per accent as the denominator of the fractions. For example, fractions expressed as fourths would use paper with 4 divisions per accent. If the data is in days of the week, use 5 divisions per accent to show 5 working days, 6 divisions per accent to show 6 working days, or 7 divisions per accent to show 7 days.

When data covers a range of more than one decimal order of magnitude (for example more than 1 to 10 or more than 10 to 100) you may wish to use a *semilog* or log grid. They show the *percentage change* rather than the *arithmetic change* of the data. More about these grids is in the logarithmic section, page 19.

Select Grid— Select a graph paper with enough graduations so you can accurately plot the data. Don't use more lines than the data requires because it makes the graph hard to read.

Scale the Grid— Scaling changes can cause many visual distortions as shown in the accompanying illustrations.

There is no firm rule as to what is correct scaling, but the general practice is to locate the lowest point on the Y axis within the bottom 20% of the graph, and the highest point within the top 20% of the graph. Try to have the plotted line at a 30° to 40° angle to the X axis.

Graph proportions are usually square or rectangular with the ratio between the sides not exceeding 7 to 10.

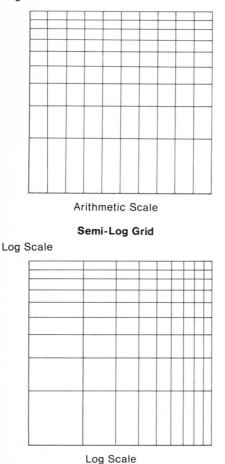

Log Scale

Arithmetic Scale

Semi-Log Grid

Log Scale

Log Scale

Log-Log Grid

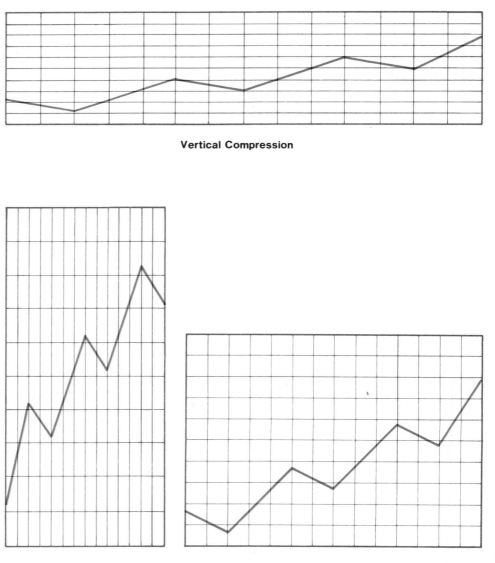

Vertical Compression

Horizontal Compression

Normal Grid

Break in Axis—Sometimes it is necessary to show small changes in data of large magnitude. This can be done by interrupting the axis with a break and showing only the top portion of the data.

Breaks distort the amount of change because they do not show a true picture of the relation of the data to the base. When you use a break, extend it all the way across the graph so it is easy to see.

Label Axes—Each axis should be clearly labeled with its numeric values and with its description, for example:

Population in Thousands
Price in $1,000
Percent
Fiscal Years

Horizontal labels are easier to read when used on both axes because you don't have to rotate the page to read them.

Multiple Scales on X & Y Axes—When multiple sets of data with different ranges are plotted on the same graph it may be necessary to use more than one scale on either the X or Y axis. Scales may be placed on the same side of the graph or on opposite sides.

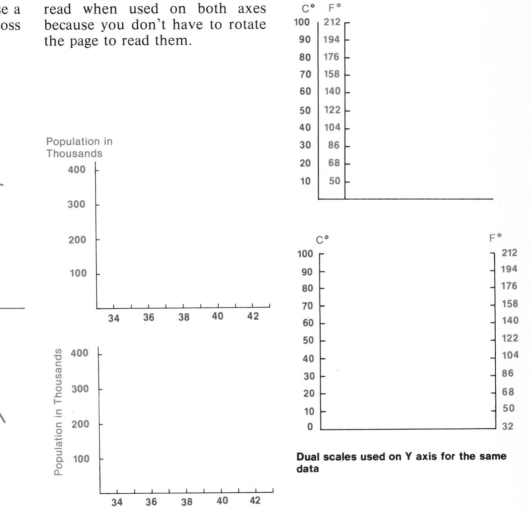

Dual scales used on Y axis for the same data

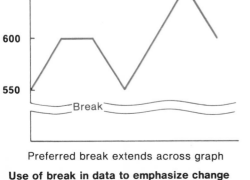

Data with no break

Enlarged scale with break

Preferred break extends across graph

Use of break in data to emphasize change

However, vertical labels are perfectly acceptable. Although awkward for long titles, top-to-bottom labels can also be read without rotating the page.

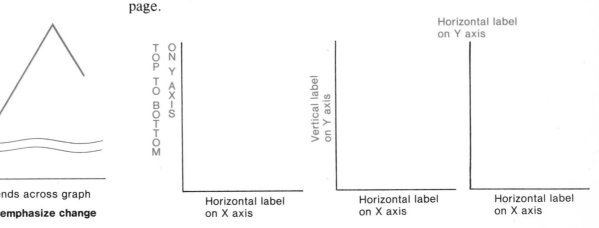

You may also use more than one scale on the X axis to show days, weeks and months.

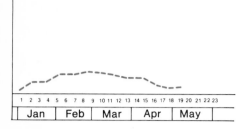

Weekly and monthly scale on X axis

Use more than one scale on the same graph where the two scales represent different but related data. This is useful for showing related information such as dollar sales and unit sales or purchasing power of the dollar in percent and gross national product in dollars.

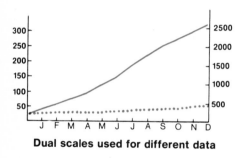

Dual scales used for different data

Z Graphs—Where the graph shows a *current status*, a *cumulative status* and a *moving average* it is called a *Z graph*. These are used to show economic and business trends and data comparison on a year-to-date basis.

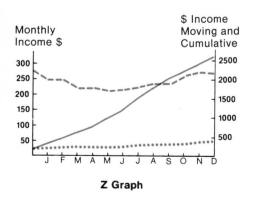

Z Graph

When you want to make a master graph, type the graph title on an adhesive label.

Multiple-Curve Graphs—When you want to compare the data from several years, you may superimpose the curves on the same graph. When you do this, January of the first year will be on the same division line as January of the second year and so on. Each curve must be identified. This type of graph is called a *multiple-curve graph*.

Multiple-curve graphs with curves approaching or crossing each other should have each curve labeled for clarity. Colors may be used, but when copied, all colors will reproduce as black on most copiers. A better choice is to use different types of lines for each curve: One can be a solid line, one can be broken into dashes or dots, another can be a combination of dashes and dots. Colors can be applied to each of the curves on each copy of the graph if you want to make each curve highly visible for emphasis.

Title the Graph—Where possible, titles should read parallel to the X axis so they are easily read without turning the page. Each graph should have a full title. It is usually placed at the top of the graph, at

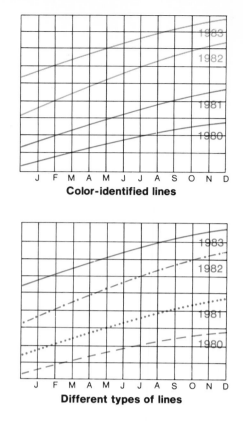

Color-identified lines

Different types of lines

the bottom of the graph or in a block inset within the graph. If you are working directly on graph paper, a block inset is easily accomplished by applying an adhesive label over the section where you wish the title. You may want to type or letter the label before applying it to the graph.

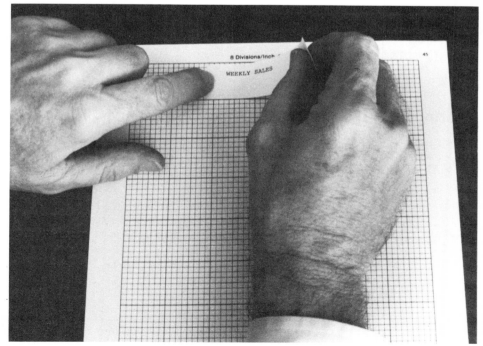

Plot Data Points—Using data from the table on page 7, use a pencil to plot the first data point at its X and Y coordinates.

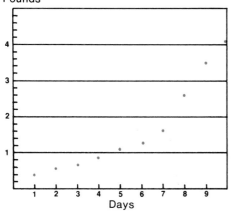

WEIGHT GAIN OVER TIME

Plot all data points on the graph. Examine the graph to see if there are unusual variations in the points plotted. If there are any, double-check them against the data to make sure there are no plotting errors. Corrections are easy to make while all of the points are still in pencil.

When the X axis represents time, plot data on the line which represents the *end* of the time period.

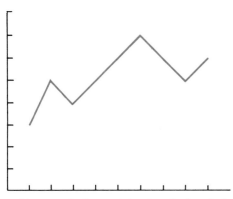

Line graph shows data at end of period

If you are making a bar graph, the space between lines indicates the time period *ending* with the line indicated on the X axis.

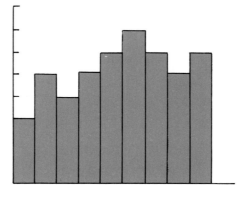

Bar graph shows data in the period before end of line

Connect Data Points—Draw a line to connect each point you have plotted. You can use a ruler to form a series of straight lines or a French curve to draw a curved line. Lines connecting data points on a graph are usually called *curves* even if they are straight lines.

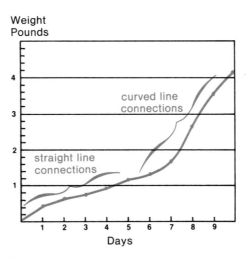

Data points may be connected with straight lines or a French curve

The line may be smoothed by connecting extreme peaks; by drawing the line to approximate the location of the data points rather than exactly to them; or by using a *moving average* as described on page 13.

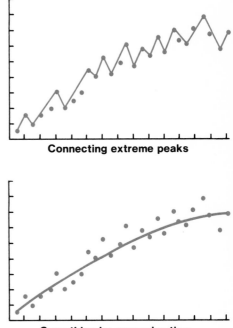

Connecting extreme peaks

Smoothing by approximation

If more than one line is to be drawn on the graph, first plot all the points for one line and then draw it—and so on for each additional line.

When you draw more than one line or curve on the same graph, use the following types of lines:

——————————— Primary data
– – – – – – – – – Secondary data
. . . . Tertiary data

Where more than three sets of data are presented, use lighter versions of these lines.

——————— Primary data
— — — — — — Secondary data
. . . . Tertiary data

or combinations

— —— — —— — Primary data
— — — — — — — Secondary data
— — — . — — — Tertiary data

Do not use heavy dots on lines unless they represent data points.

Identifying Data Points—It is often desirable to identify each plotted point with a small dot for later reference. Further identification may be added by writing the value of the point next to it where it will not interfere with the plotted line. If you want to show the range of the data that occurred in the period before the graph began, use a vertical bar along the left side of the graph.

PLOTTING DATA WITH EXTREME VARIATIONS

Plotting a series of data points often produces a graph with such extreme variations that the meaning of the data is obscured.

Generally, extreme variation can be reduced by using a broader data base. For example, if day-to-day variation is too extreme, plotting weekly totals of the same data will usually produce less variation and plotting monthly totals further reduces the variation.

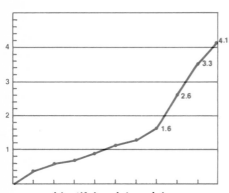

Identifying data points

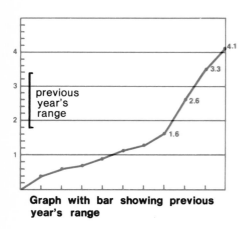

Graph with bar showing previous year's range

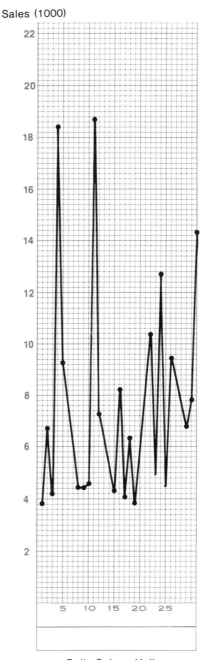

Daily Sales—Units

Graph showing extreme variation

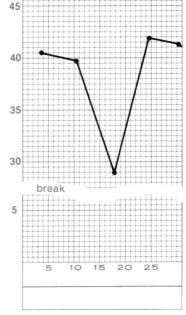

Weekly Sales—Units

Graph is smoothed by plotting a longer time interval

When it is important to show quantitative amounts, plot the *daily arithmetic average* of the data for that week or that month. The daily arithmetic average is easily calculated by adding the data for the week and dividing the total by the number of days data was generated that week.

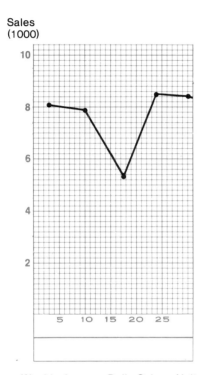

Weekly Average Daily Sales—Units

Quantitative Relationship Shown by Average Daily Sales

MOVING AVERAGE

The preceding techniques reduce data variation by plotting a group of data, and so reduce the number of points shown. When it is desirable to reduce data variation and still plot one point for each data sample, you use a moving average.

Here is an example of a 5-day moving average: The first 5 days' sales of 3,800, 6,400, 4,200, 18,400, and 9,000, are totaled. The sum of 41,800 is divided by 5. This 8,300 average is plotted at day 3, the center point of the 5 days. The same is done for days 2 through 6, and the result is plotted at day 4.

You can use any time period for the average: 5 days, 10 days, a month or a year. It takes a little experimentation to find out what time period works best for a particular problem.

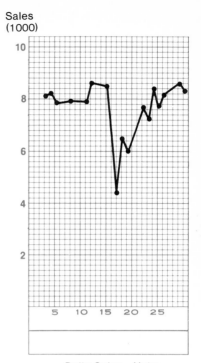

Daily Sales—Units
5-Day Moving Average

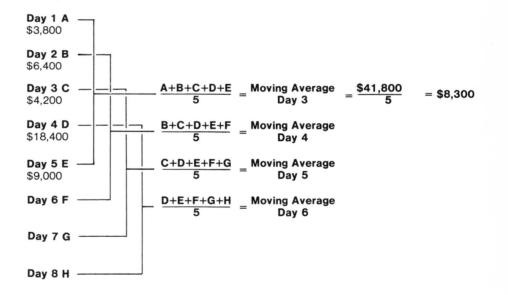

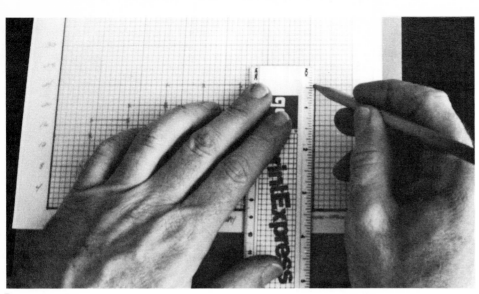

By tracing the graph onto tracing paper you can remove unnecessary lines and make the graph cleaner and easier to understand.

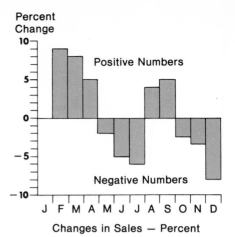

Negative Numbers on a bar graph

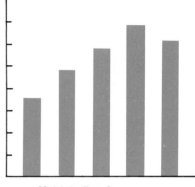

Multiple Bar Graph

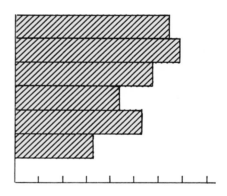

Bar graphs can be drawn horizontally

TRACING A GRAPH

You may want to make a graph with no grid lines. First draw the graph on a copied graph, then trace it on plain paper. Copy only the parts you want to show. You may want to include X and Y axes.

When tracing, allow adequate space to the left and bottom for vertical and horizontal scales.

Because the grid will not show on your traced copy, you will have to provide calibration and labeling. This may be done in three ways: ruling the most significant horizontal and vertical lines, using *tick marks* on the most significant horizontal and vertical lines, or using *rulings* for the major-significant horizontal and vertical lines and using *tick marks* for the less-significant horizontal and vertical lines.

PLOTTING DATA

Data points should be plotted on X-axis lines representing the end of the time period, except on bar charts. Bar charts should show each bar in the space before the division line showing the end of the data period. Data should be plotted in pencil first, then drawn in ink.

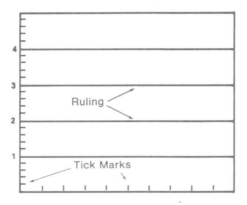

Use of tick marks and ruling

You may want to eliminate horizontal and vertical lines in the area where there is no data. This uncluttered area can be used for titles and explanations.

BAR GRAPHS

Bar graphs show one or more bars, the parts or length of which show data size. They are similar to line graphs except that individual bars are drawn vertically from the X axis to the data point, rather than connecting the data points with a line.

Bar graphs may also be drawn with horizontal bars originating from the Y axis.

Negative numbers may be shown on bar graphs by showing the bar below the X axis or to the left of the Y axis.

Division lines are not needed between bars. Tick marks or a minimum of division lines are needed on the other axis to show the bar lengths.

When bars originate from the X axis and show time, bar width shows the period covered by the data. The right side of the bar indicates the end of the period.

Bar graphs may be used to show data or percentages. They should always originate from zero unless they are drawn on a log scale.

SINGLE BAR GRAPHS

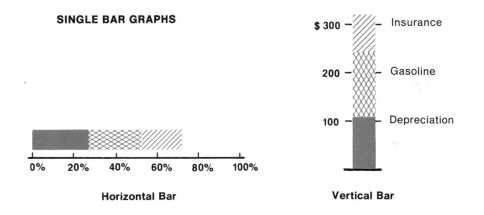

Horizontal Bar

$ 300 — Insurance

200 — Gasoline

100 — Depreciation

Vertical Bar

DATA SOURCE
  All graphs should note data source, time, location, and other pertinent information.

Identifying Data

Bars may be solid or shaded for identification of data. The illustration shows preferred shading patterns for bar graphs.

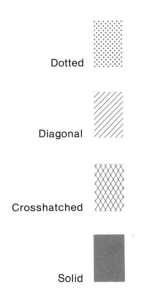

Dotted

Diagonal

Crosshatched

Solid

Component or segmented-bar graphs show component parts and make comparisons in the manner of the surface graph. Single-component bar graphs are used like pie graphs. They should show the largest data on the bottom with the heaviest shading. As you move upward showing data in decreasing order of size, use progressively lighter shading.

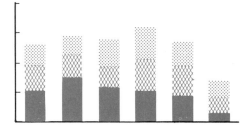

Component or Segmented Bar Graph

Shaded tapes and rub-on transfer materials are sold at art, blueprint and office-supply stores for this purpose.

Identification of shadings may be given in a separate box rather than on the graph itself.

Multiple-bar graphs are used to make comparisons of data points.

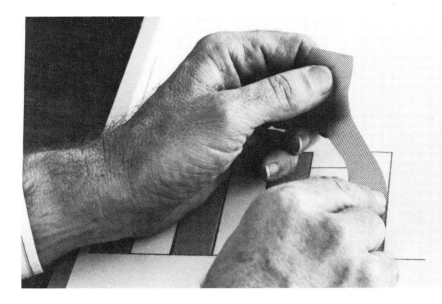

Self-adhesive patterned tape, which is available in a variety of sizes and designs from art-supply stores, will improve the graphic message of any bar graph.

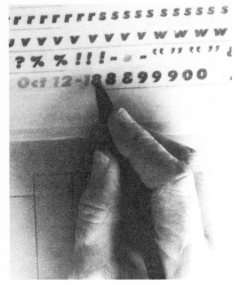

A good burnishing tool for rub-on transfers is the cap of a ball-point pen.

THERMOMETER GRAPH

The thermometer graph is often used to represent achievement of goals. It allows plotting percentage elements less than or greater than 100%. It also provides a convenient way to present quantitative and percentage information in highly effective visual form.

The same shading and identification rules for bar graphs are used for thermometer graphs. In fact, a thermometer graph is a single bar graph with a bulb on the bottom. You can plot quantities greater than 100% by extending the graph above the 100% mark.

Thermometer graphs can also be shown horizontally.

PIE GRAPHS

A *pie graph* (named after the dessert, not the Greek letter) is a circle divided into segments representing its components. It is another way to illustrate percentage distribution. A pie graph is a circle with the circumference representing 100%. It is divided into wedges representing percentages of a whole. Several pie graphs are on pages 79 through 81. Pick the size that will be easiest to scale.

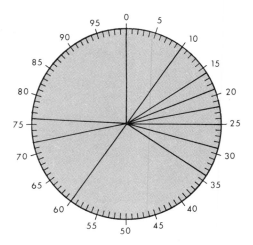

Pie Graph or Circular-Percentage Graph

Compound-bar graphs show side-by-side comparisons of data within the same group, and show side-by-side comparison of groups.

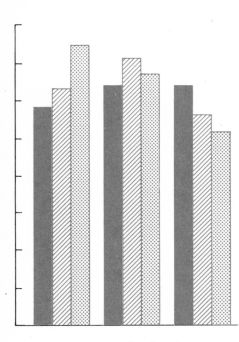

Compound Bar Graph

Thermometer Graph

The best way to make a pie graph is to prepare a table listing the items to be shown on the graph. Use this table to calculate the percentage of the total each item represents. Mark these percentages around the circumference and draw lines from the centerpoint to the circumference to form wedges showing percentages.

Percentage marks around the graph may be covered with opaque white correction fluid or left in place. You may label each wedge with the percentage or amount it represents—or both—with its title. Make your graph copies easier to read by coloring or shading each wedge.

There are two major limitations of the pie graph. It can only represent a static moment in time and it cannot exceed 100%.

SCALES

A vertical scale should be fine enough so it is easy to make and read the chart. The horizontal scale should be appropriate for the data used, for example, days or weeks.

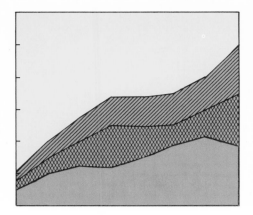

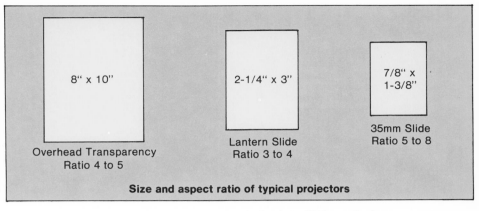

Size and aspect ratio of typical projectors

If the graph is to be projected, size it to fit the projector.

SURFACE GRAPHS

Surface graphs show data size by the relative amount of surface between two lines. They are similar to line graphs except they have more than one line. The top line represents the cumulative total. Each of the lines below it represents a part of the total amount. The same shading patterns used for bar graphs are used for surface graphs.

GEOGRAPHIC DISTRIBUTION GRAPHS

The geographic distribution graph is an outline map used to show data locations plotted on the map. Typical geographic distribution graphs include weather or population distribution.

Geographic graphs can be combined with pie or bar graphs to show distribution of relative quantities. Applications include plotting geographic information such as airline routes or sales territories.

REPORTS

If the graph is a part of a report, try to position the graph so it is not necessary to rotate the page to read it. If it is necessary to rotate the page, the graph should read correctly when you rotate the page a quarter turn clockwise.

Geographic Distribution Graph

LOGARITHMS AND HOW THEY WORK

An arithmetic graph shows the *amount of change*. A logarithmic graph shows the *percent of change* or *ratio of change*.

Like stairway steps, the change between each number in an *arithmetic progression* is always the same. It can be 1 as in

1 2 3 4 5 6 ...

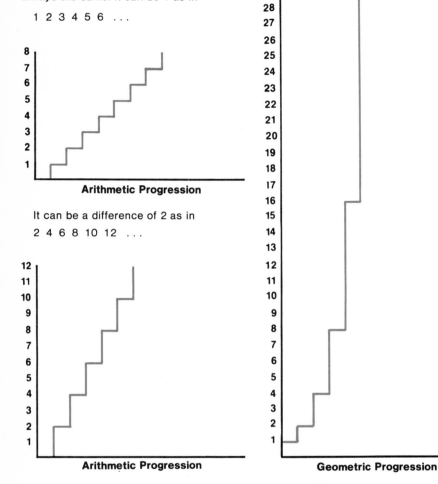

Arithmetic Progression

It can be a difference of 2 as in

2 4 6 8 10 12 ...

Arithmetic Progression

Geometric Progression

In a *geometric progression*, the size of each step varies but the *percent* of change is constant. Thus in the following geometric progression, each step is multiplied by 2 to find the value of the next step.

2 4 8 16 32 64 ...

The multiplier can be 5 or 10 or 50 or any other number, *but the change is always the same.*

Here's a geometric progression with 10 as the multiplier:

10 100 1,000 10,000
100,000 1,000,000 ...

The progression 2, 4, 8, 16, 32, 64 can also be written as

2^1 2^2 2^3 2^4 2^5 2^6 ...

and the progression 10, 100, 1,000, 10,000, 100,000, 1,000,000 ... can be written as

10^1 10^2 10^3 10^4 10^5 10^6 ...

The small number at the top right is called an *exponent*. The large number is called the *base*, thus when 1,000 is written as

10^3

10 is the base and ^{3} is the exponent. The exponent is the number of times the base number is multiplied by itself to produce the number. Thus 10^3 is the same as 10 x 10 x 10, which is 1,000.

Before the development of slide rules and digital calculators, mathematicians took advantage of the fact that numbers can be multiplied by each other by expressing them as a base with an exponent and then adding the exponents. The exponent is called a *logarithm*.

The *common* logarithm (log) of a number is the *exponent* to the base ten of that number—that is, the number of times ten is multiplied by itself to make that number. Thus the common logarithm 2 means 10 x 10 or 10^2 and equals 100. The following table shows a list of the simple powers or exponents of 10 and their logarithms:

Number	Power	Logarithm
0.001	10^{-3}	-3
0.01	10^{-2}	-2
0.1	10^{-1}	-1
1	10^{-0}	0
10	10^{-1}	1
100	10^{-2}	2
1,000	10^{-3}	3
10,000	10^{-4}	4
100,000	10^{-5}	5

Adding the exponents of numbers causes the base numbers (the 10 in this case) to be multiplied. Thus 10^2 x 10^3 = 10^5, or expressing it another way—100 x 1,000 = 100,000.

Now let's do the same thing in logarithms. The table shows the log of 100 is 2 and the log of 1,000 is 3. When you add the logs 2 and 3, the total log is 5. In the table, log 5 is the same as the number 100,000 which is the same as the product of 100 x 1,000.

Division may be accomplished by subtracting the logarithm of one number from that of another and looking up the number represented by the resulting logarithm. For example Log 4 minus Log 2 = Log 2 = 10,000 ÷ 100 = 100.

Numbers between 1 and 10 have logarithms between 0 and 1. They are expressed as decimals. Tables of logarithms expressed as decimals, sometimes to ten or more places, are in many technical books. You can buy books devoted solely to tables of logarithms. This table shows the common logarithms or exponents to the base 10 of the numbers from 1 to 10 rounded to 4 places:

Number	Logarithm
1	0.0000
2	0.3010
3	0.4771
4	0.6021
5	0.6990
6	0.7782
7	0.8451
8	0.9031
9	0.9542
10	1.0000

To use this table, look up the logarithms of two numbers. Add the logarithms together to find the logarithm of their product. Look up the logarithm to find their product. Thus the logarithm, or *log,* of 2 is 0.3010 and the log of 3 is 0.4771. Adding the log of 2 and the log of 3 (0.3010 + 0.4771) gives 0.7782. When you find this number in the preceding table, you will see that 0.7782 is the log of 6, which is the product of 2 x 3. Thus, adding the logs of two numbers is the same as multiplying those two numbers.

GRAPH PAPER From Your COPIER—**HPBooks**

LOG GRAPHS

A logarithmic graph shows *percentage change*, not *arithmetic change*. A certain distance on the scale at any location represents the same percentage change as that distance at any other location on the scale. Because log-graph paper shows percentage change, it is sometimes called *ratio paper*.

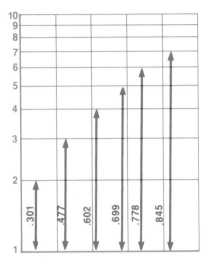

Position of numbers on log scale

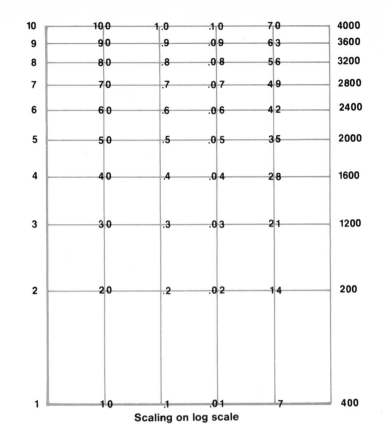

Scaling on log scale

To make a logarithmic graph, a log scale is laid out so the distance between 1 and 2 is equal to 0.3010 of the distance from 1 to 10; the distance from 1 to 3 is 0.4771 of the distance 1 to 10. The log of 3 is 0.4771, the scale position of 3 is placed 4771/10,000 of the distance between 1 and 10, and so on. Each step gets smaller and smaller.

A log scale has no zero because the scale progresses upward by multiplication and downward by division, rather than by addition and subtraction. Each log scale is called a *cycle*. Where two cycles are put end to end, the scale is called a *two-cycle scale*. When three cycles are used, it is called a *three-cycle scale*, and so on.

Each cycle represents a change from log 0 to log +1 or 10^0 to 10^1. Because it shows a change of 10 times the starting number, it can show the change from 1 to 10, or 10 to 100, or 100 to 1,000. It can also show the change from 0.1 to 1 or 0.01 to 0.1. Any convenient number can be assigned to the base line.

A two-cycle scale represents the change from 10^0 to 10^2 or 1 to 100—a change of 100. A three-cycle scale represents a change from 10^0 to 10^3 or 1 to 1,000—a change of 1,000.

You can multiply the numbers on a log scale by any number or decimal you wish. For example, the scale can be 1 to 10, 4 to 40 or 60 to 600.

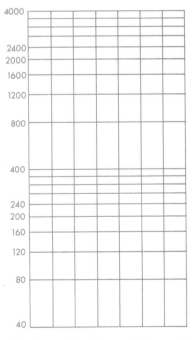

2-Cycle Log Scale　　　　**How to scale a two-cycle log grid**

Numbering—Semi-log graphs are numbered on the right as a guide and to allow room for labeling on the left. Log-log graphs are numbered on the top and on the right as a guide and to allow room for labeling on the bottom and to the left.

PLOTTING PERCENTAGES ON LOG GRAPHS

The distance from 10 to 20 is 0.3010 of the distance from 10 to 100. The distance from 40 to 80 is also 0.3010 of the distance from 10 to 100. The increase from 10 to 20 and 20 to 40 are both increases of 100%. Any change of 100% will occur over the same distance anywhere on the graph.

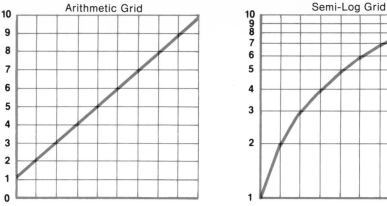

Arithmetic progression on arithmetic and semi-log grids

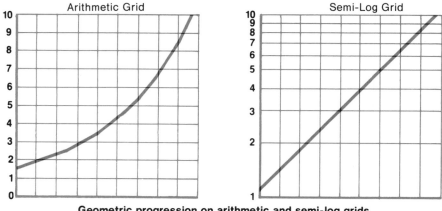

Geometric progression on arithmetic and semi-log grids

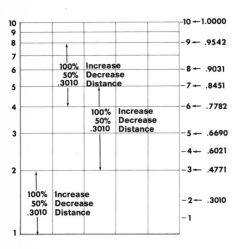

Percentage change on log scale

In the same manner, any percentage change—say 30%—will occupy the same distance as any other 30% change.

Logarithmic graph paper, called *log paper* for short, or sometimes *ratio paper*, is available for both types of graphs and I have included both kinds in this book.

Graphs which cover a range of one decimal order of magnitude (10 to 100, 10^1 to 10^2 or Log 1 to Log 2) are called *single-cycle*. Graphs covering a change of two decimal orders of magnitude from 1 to 1,000—Log 1 to Log 3, are called *two-cycle*, and so on.

This book provides semi-log graphs with 1 to 10 cycles. It also provides log-log graphs with 1 to 10 cycles on the X axis, each with 1 to 10 cycles on the Y axis.

When you plot a geometric progression on a log scale it becomes a straight line, but when you plot an arithmetic progression on a log scale it becomes a curved line.

Arithmetic graphs measure *arithmetic* change. Log graphs measure *percentage* change. They are also used to compress data to show a wide range of data in a small space. A 5-cycle log graph can show a range of 100,000 numbers—difficult to do on an arithmetic graph if you want the graph to show small numbers.

Log scales are used on two types of graphs:

Those which compare a percentage change with an arithmetic change such as time are called *semi-log* or *single-axis* graphs. These graphs have a logarithmic scale on one axis and an arithmetic scale on the other axis.

Those which compare percentage change with another percentage change are called *log-log* graphs or *dual-axis* graphs. These graphs have logarithmic scales on both axes.

HOW TO USE LOG GRAPHS

To use log graphs, first examine the range of data to determine the number of decimal orders of magnitude of change and thus the number of logarithmic cycles you will need.

Decide what number you wish to start with at the bottom of the graph—not zero.

Write that number at the bottom tick mark for the first cycle. Write 10 times that number at the top tick mark of the second cycle, 100 times that number at the top tick mark of the third cycle, and so on.

Repeat for the other axis of the graph if it is also a log axis. If not, the spacing between grid lines on that axis will be uniform and you must assign units based on an arithmetic progression.

When tracing a graph from log paper, major accent lines must be retained and identified. Unaccented or minor accent lines may be replaced by tick marks or eliminated.

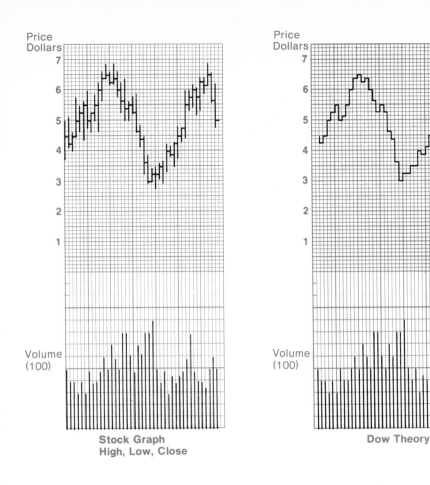

Stock Graph
High, Low, Close

Dow Theory

POINT-AND-FIGURE GRAPHS

Point-and-figure graphs use a series of X's to indicate price trend. An X may indicate any price range you choose, for example, 1 point, 7 points or 3 points.

In a 1-point graph, the paper is scaled on the Y axis so one square equals one point. An X is placed on the square showing the present price. When the price has advanced or declined to the next even full point, a second X is placed in the same column above or below the last X. When the price changes in the other direction by one full point, an X is placed on the stock price in the next column to the right. X's are continued in this column until the price changes in the other direction. Some analysts use X's in the columns when price is increasing and O's when the price is decreasing.

Point-and-figure graphs are used to show stock-price *trends*. They do not show volume, nor do they show the price on any given date.

STOCK-MARKET GRAPHS

Stock-market graphs often have two grids with a common time scale on the X axis: one showing price and the other showing volume. Volume is shown as a series of vertical bars along the bottom of a small graph accented in tenths. Because stock is traded in eighths of a point, the upper grid is accented in eighths. There are several ways to plot price on this grid. Most common is a vertical bar between the high price and the low price of the day, with a horizontal tick to the right showing the closing price for that day.

Individual stocks may be plotted on arithmetic grids, or on semi-log grids to show percentage change. When a stock and an indicator such as the Dow-Jones average are plotted on the same grid, a semi-log grid must be used because relative change is implied.

DOW THEORY

Followers of the Dow Theory use a step chart to indicate price change. They plot closing prices as a series of horizontal lines. These lines are connected by vertical lines forming a series of steps. The result is similar to the previous method, but does not show price extremes during the day.

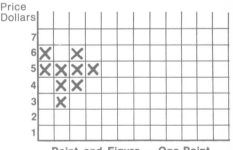

Point-and-Figure — One Point

LINES
Lines connecting data points should be bold enough to stand out on the graph. Lines should be identified on multiple-curve graphs.

PROBABILITY GRAPHS

A probability graph shows what has occurred in the past and what will probably happen in the future, assuming the past is a model of the future.

The principle of the probability graph is based on the theory that plotting any series of natural occurrences will form a *normal distribution* or "bell-shaped" curve. For example, if you measured the circumference of the heads of a large group of boys from 16- to 19- years old, you would find a distribution similar to that shown by Winfield S. Hall in his article *The Evaluation of Anthropometric Data.**

* Page 1646, Vol. 37, *Journal of the American Medical Association.*

HEAD SIZES OF 1071 BOYS AGES 16 TO 19

Head Circum- ference (cm)	Number of Boys	Percent of Total	Cumula- tive Percent
51	4	.0037	.0037
52	23	.0214	.0251
53	59	.0550	.0801
54	108	.1008	.1809
55	224	.2092	.3901
56	257	.2400	.6301
57	230	.2148	.8449
58	110	.1027	.9476
59	38	.0355	.9831
60	16	.0149	.9980
61	2	.0020	1.0000
Total	1,071		

The Bell-Shaped Curve—When a curve is drawn plotting the number, or percentage occurrence, of boys with each head size, it forms a "bell-shaped" curve as shown in the illustration.

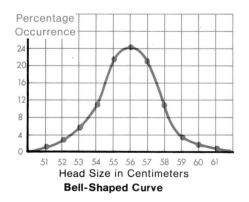

Bell-Shaped Curve

By dividing the number of boys with each head size by the total

number of boys, you will arrive at the percentage distribution shown in the table. Obtain the cumulative percentage for each head size by adding the percent of total for each size to all the percent of totals for all smaller sizes. This is shown in the last column of the table.

Ogive—When this *cumulative percent* is plotted on the Y axis, it forms an S-shape curve called an *ogive.* Plotting this curve with the cumulative percentage on the X axis reverses the curve.

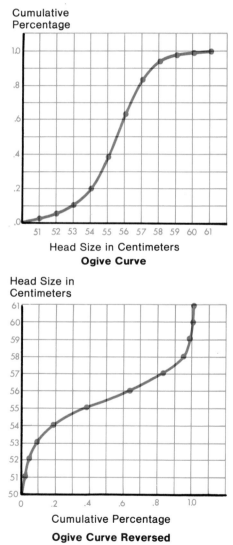

Ogive Curve

Ogive Curve Reversed

Probability Grid—If you draw a grid in which the Y axis is an arithmetic scale, and the X axis shows the distance between percentages, you have a grid which will produce a straight line when the ogive is drawn. This grid is similar to that of the probability papers in this book.

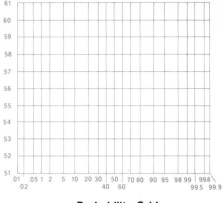

Probability Grid

When you plot a series of known points on this grid and they form a straight line, this line can be projected to estimate the probability of future occurrence.

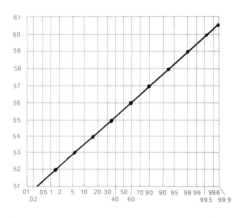

Probability grid with percentage of head size plotted

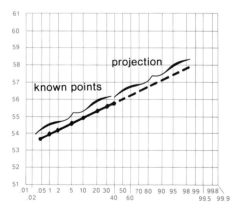

Projection of known data on probability grid to predict occurrences

The accuracy of this projection will depend on how straight the line is, and the size of the data sample. More information about this subject can be found in any book on statistics under *probabilities, standard deviation, skewing,* and *kurtosis.*

The vertical scale of most probability paper is arithmetic. However, log-scale probability paper is used where the probability on the X axis is the probability of a percentage function (log function) on the Y axis.

ERRORS

Errors are readily corrected and unwanted material eliminated by using opaque white correction fluid that will not reproduce when copies of the graph are made. Two types of correction fluid are available. The most common type for correcting typing allows some copy toner to bleed through the correction. Correction fluid designed for correcting copies allows less toner bleed-through. It may be necessary to apply more than one coat of correction fluid to blank out errors or unwanted material.

WHEN YOU NEED LARGER PAPER

When a larger sheet of graph paper is required, smaller sheets may be put together by trimming the bottom margin of one sheet and splicing it to the preceding sheet. If the axis is arithmetic, the top sheet may be overlapped and V's cut in the top and bottom of the grid to facilitate horizontal and vertical alignment.

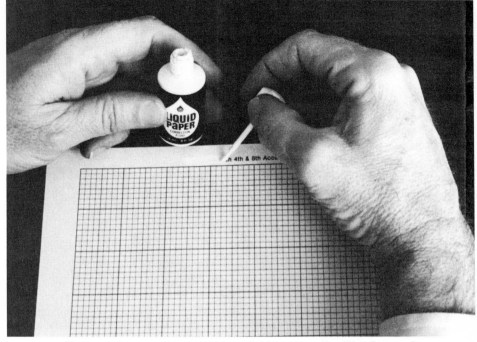

You can also use white correction fluid to cover the title of a graph.

By splicing copies together, you can make any size graph you need.

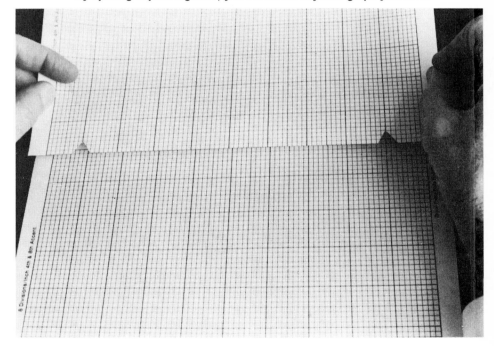

BIBLIOGRAPHY

American National Standards Institute, Inc. *Illustrations for Publication and Projection*, New York: The American Society of Mechanical Engineers, 1959.

Arkin H., and Colton, R. R. *Graphs: And How to Make and Use Them*, New York: Harper and Brothers, 1939.

Brinton, W. C. *Graphic Methods of Presenting Facts*, New York: McGraw-Hill Book Co., 1914.

Brinton, W.C. *Graphic Presentation*, New York: Brinton Associates, 1939.

Bruins, T. A. *The Ratio Chart in Business*, Norwood, Mass: Codex Book Co., 1926.

Carsten, K. G. *Charts and Graphs*, New York: Prentice-Hall, Inc., 1923.

Chaney, W. L. " Comparison of 'Arithmetic' and 'Ratio' Charts," *Monthly Labor Review*, Vol. VIII, No. 3, (March, 1919), pp. 20—34.

Croxton, F. E., and Cowden, D. J. *Applied General Statistics*, New York: Prentice-Hall, Inc., 1939.

Fischel, Irving. "The 'Ratio' Chart for Plotting Statistics," *Quarterly Publication of the American Statistical Association*, Vol. 15, No. 117, (June, 1917), pp. 577—601.

Funkhauser, H. G., and Walker, H. M. "Playfair and his Charts," *Economic History*, (February 1935), pp. 103—109.

Haskell, A. C. *Graphic Charts in Business*, Norwood, Mass.: Codex Book Co., 1928.

Katzenberg, A. C. *How to Draw Graphs*, Kalamazoo, Mich.: Behaviordelia, Inc., 1975.

Modley, R. *How to Use Pictorial Statistics*, New York: McGraw-Hill Book Co., 1936.

Mudgett, B. D. *Statistical Tables and Graphs*, Boston, Mass.: Houghton Mifflin Co., 1930.

Riggleman, J. R. *Graphic Methods for Presenting Business Statistics*, New York: McGraw-Hill Book Co., 1936.

Selby, Peter W. *Using Graphs and Tables, a Self-Teaching Guide*, New York: John Wiley & Sons, Inc., 1979.

Subcommittee on Preferred Practice in Graphic Presentation, *Code of Preferred Practice for Graphic Presentation and The Series Charts*, New York: American Society of Mechanical Engineers, 1936.

Weld, W. E. *How to Chart Facts from Figures with Graphs*, Norwood, Mass.: Codex Book Co., 1972.

Index

CIRCULAR-PERCENTAGE GRAPHS

Diameter (inches)	Page
7	79
6	80
5	81
4	81
3	80
2	80
1	81

GEOGRAPHIC DISTRIBUTION

TIME SERIES ARITHMETIC GRIDS
(Note: for Semi-Log Time Series see Semi-Log Grids)

Time on Short Axis

X AXIS	Y AXIS		Page
	Divisions	Accent	
1 Day by 1/2 Hour	100	5 & 10	97
1 Month by Days	100	5 & 10	98
1 Year by Weeks	100	5 & 10	99
1 Year by Months	120	10	100
3 Years by Months	100	5 & 10	101
5 Years by Months	170	5 & 10	102
10 Years by Months	100	5 & 10	103

Stock Market

X AXIS	Divisions	Accent	Page
13 Weeks by 6 Day	25 point	1/4 point Division (100 Div Accent 4)	104
27 Weeks by 5 Day	25 point	1/8 point Division (100 Div Accent 8)	105
27 Weeks by 6 Day	20 point	1/8 point Division (162 Div Accent 4 with volume scale)	106

Time on Long Axis

X AXIS	Divisions	Accent	Page
1 Day by 1/4 Hour	100	5	107
1 Day by 1/2 Hour	100	5 & 10	108
5 Days by Hour	70	5 & 10	109
6 Months by Days	120	10	110
1 Year by Days	250	5 & 10	111
1 Year by Months	100	5 & 10	112
5 Years by Months	100	5 & 10	113

SEMI-LOG GRIDS
X Axis in Short Direction

X Axis Division	X Axis Accent	Application	Y Axis—Number of Log Cycles 1	2	3	4	5	6	7	8	10
12	None	Hours/Year by Month	114	115	117	118					
31	None	Month by Days			120						
36	None	3 Years by Month			121						
52	None	Year by Weeks		123	125						
60	6	Hour by Min/5 Years by Month	126	128	129	130					
70	5, 10	1/10 1/2 and 1"	131	132	133	134	135	136	137	138	139
84	6, 12	Hours/7 Years by Month	140	141	142	143	144				
84	7	Days per Week	145	146	147	148	149	150			
90	5, 10	2 Millimeters/Div	151	152	153	154	155	156			
120	5, 10	Time			157	158	159	160	161		
180	5, 10	1, 5, 10 Millimeters	163	164	165	166	167	168	169	170	171

SEMI-LOG GRIDS
X Axis in Long Direction

X Axis Division	X Axis Accent	Application	Y Axis—Number of Log Cycles 1	2
12	None	Hours/Year by Month		116
31	None	Month by Days		119
36	None	3 Years by Month		122
52	None	Year by Weeks		124
60	None	Hour by Min/5 Years by Month	127	
180	5, 10		162	
366	5th mo	Year by Days	172	

Note: Semi-Log Grids are numbered on the right as a guide and to allow room for labeling on the left.

LOG-LOG GRIDS

X Axis Cycles	Y Axis—Number of Log Cycles 1	2	3	4	5	6	8	10
1	173	174	175					
2	176	177	178	179	180			
3	181	182	183	184	185			
4		186	187	188		189		
5		190	191		192			
6				193		194	195	
8						196		197
10							198	

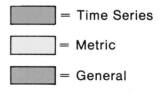

= Time Series
= Metric
= General

Note: Log-Log Grids are numbered on the top and on the right as a guide and to allow room for labeling on the bottom and to the left.

THREE-DIMENSIONAL GRID

	Divisions	Page
Isometric	5mm	199
	4/inch	200
	20mm	201
	30mm	202
Isometric Orthographic	4/inch 30°	203
	4/inch 60°	204
	2/div/cm 60°	205
Hypometric	—	206
Perspective	12 x 12 x 8 Box	207
	12 x 31 x 10 Open	208
Triangular Coordinate	—	209

POLAR-COORDINATE GRIDS

RADIUS GRADUATION			CIRCUMFERENCE GRADUATION			
Units		Accent	5°	1° Accent 5-15°	1° Accent 10°	2° Accent 10°
Min	Max					
7	10	—	210			
20	20	5		211		
35	50	5			212	
45	55	5				213
50	70	5				214
90	125	5-10				215

PROBABILITY GRIDS

X Axis— Arithmetic Divisions	Y Axis—Log							Probability	Permille	Weibull	Poisson
	40	80	90	100	1 cycle	2 cycle	3 cycle				
Probability	216	217	218	219	220	221	222	223			
Extreme Probability Log Scale						224					
Probability with Probit						225					
150 Div											226
80 Div									227		
2 cycle Log										228	
3 cycle Log								229		230	231

Binomial probability—Page 232

Index

Index

Index

Index

1/2 Day by 1/4 Hour

12:00						
12:15						
12:30						
12:45						
1:00						
1:15						
1:30						
1:45						
2:00						
2:15						
2:30						
2:45						
3:00						
3:15						
3:30						
3:45						
4:00						
4:15						
4:30						
4:45						
5:00						
5:15						
5:30						
5:45						
6:00						
6:15						
6:30						
6:45						
7:00						
7:15						
7:30						
7:45						
8:00						
8:15						
8:30						
8:45						
9:00						
9:15						
9:30						
9:45						
10:00						
10:15						
10:30						
10:45						
11:00						
11:15						
11:30						
11:45						

Day by 1/2 Hour

12:00						
12:30						
1:00						
1:30						
2:00						
2:30						
3:00						
3:30						
4:00						
4:30						
5:00						
5:30						
6:00						
6:30						
7:00						
7:30						
8:00						
8:30						
9:00						
9:30						
10:00						
10:30						
11:00						
11:30						
12:00						
12:30						
1:00						
1:30						
2:00						
2:30						
3:00						
3:30						
4:00						
4:30						
5:00						
5:30						
6:00						
6:30						
7:00						
7:30						
8:00						
8:30						
9:00						
9:30						
10:00						
10:30						
11:00						
11:30						

Week by Day

1 Month by Day (Calendar)

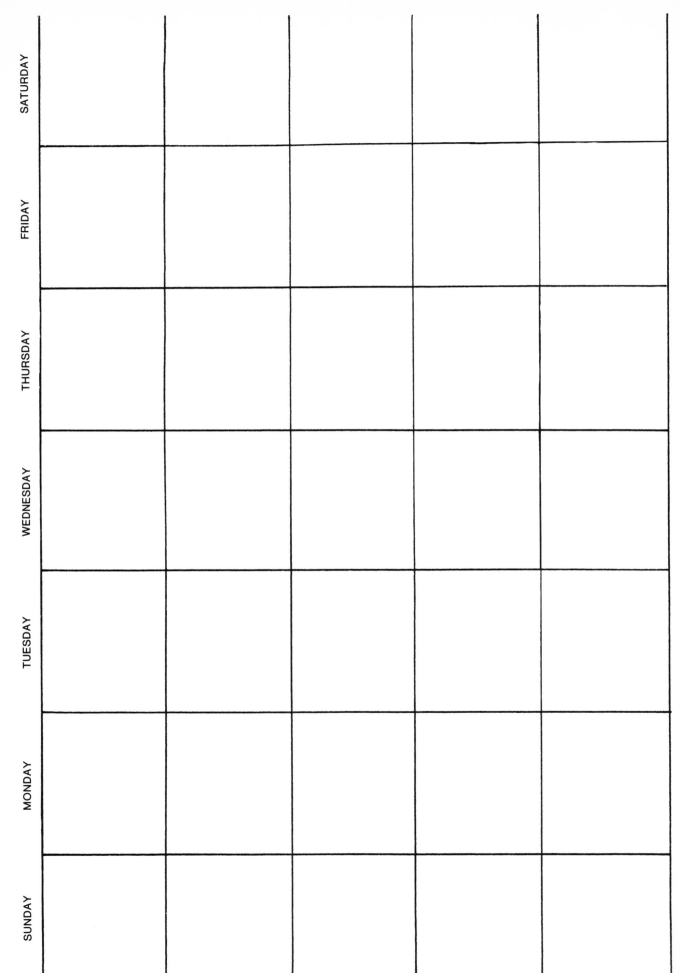

1								
2								
3								
4								
5								
6								
7								
8								
9								
10								
11								
12								
13								
14								
15								
16								
17								
18								
19								
20								
21								
22								
23								
24								
25								
26								
27								
28								
29								
30								
31								

NOTES

Year by Week

1								1
2								2
3								3
4								4
5								5
6								6
7								7
8								8
9								9
10								10
11								11
12								12
13								13
14								14
15								15
16								16
17								17
18								18
19								19
20								20
21								21
22								22
23								23
24								24
25								25
26								26
27								27
28								28
29								29
30								30
31								31
32								32
33								33
34								34
35								35
36								36
37								37
38								38
39								39
40								40
41								41
42								42
43								43
44								44
45								45
46								46
47								47
48								48
49								49
50								50
51								51
52								52
53								53

1 Year by Month

	JAN	FEB	MAR	APR	MAY	JUNE	JULY	AUG	SEPT	OCT	NOV	DEC
1												
2												
3												
4												
5												
6												
7												
8												
9												
10												
11												
12												
13												
14												
15												
16												
17												
18												
19												
20												
21												
22												
23												
24												
25												
26												
27												
28												
29												
30												
31												

3 Years by Month

	JAN	FEB	MAR	APR	MAY	JUNE	JULY	AUG	SEPT	OCT	NOV	DEC	TOTAL
	JAN	FEB	MAR	APR	MAY	JUNE	JULY	AUG	SEPT	OCT	NOV	DEC	TOTAL

GRAPH PAPER From Your COPIER—**HPBooks**

4 Divisions/Inch 4th Accent

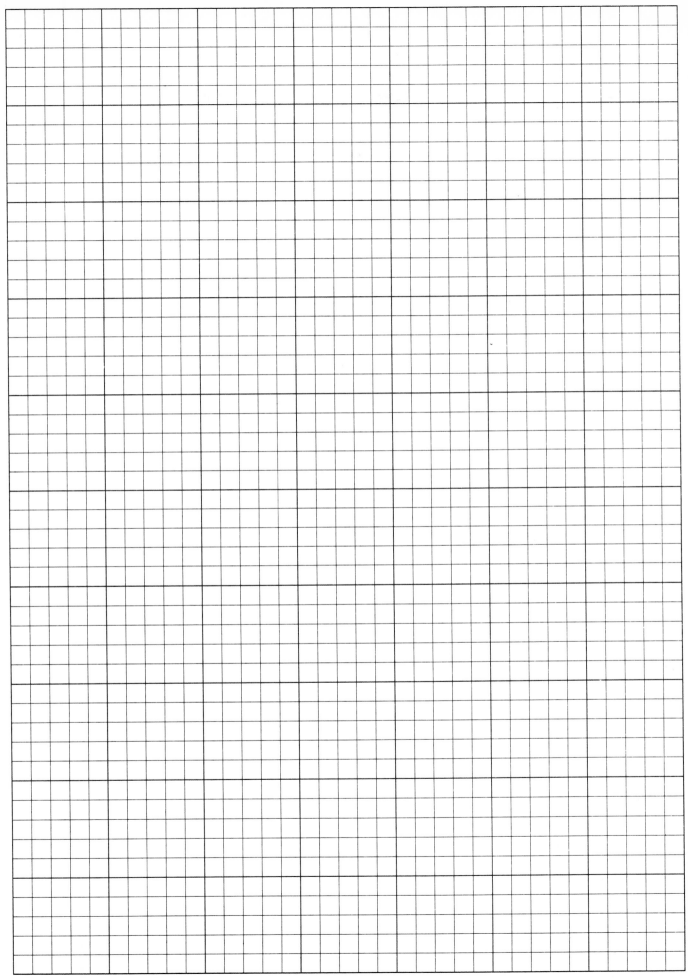

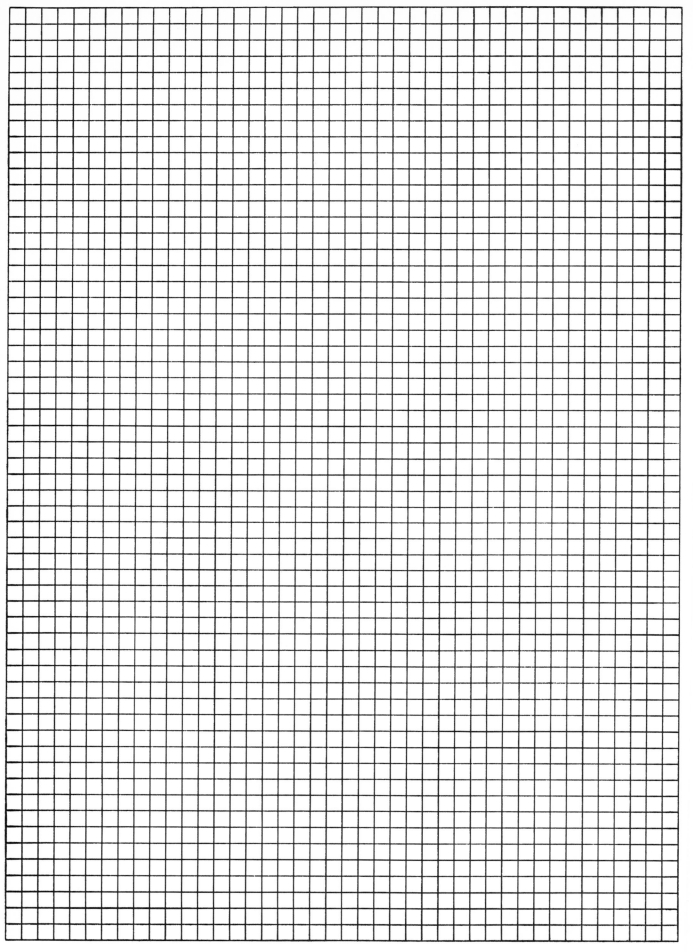

6 Divisions/Inch

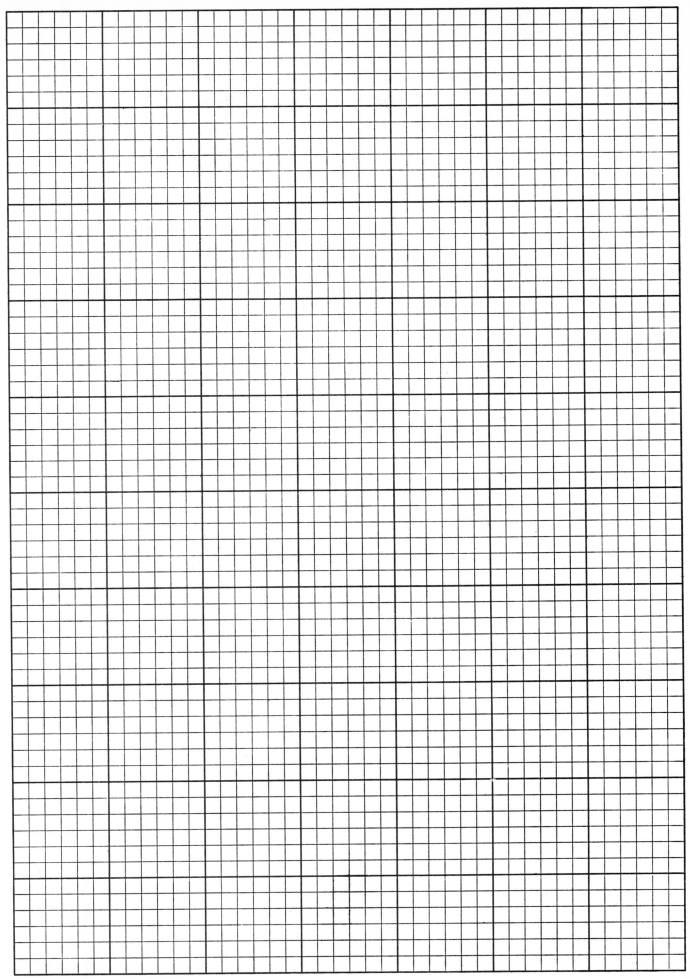

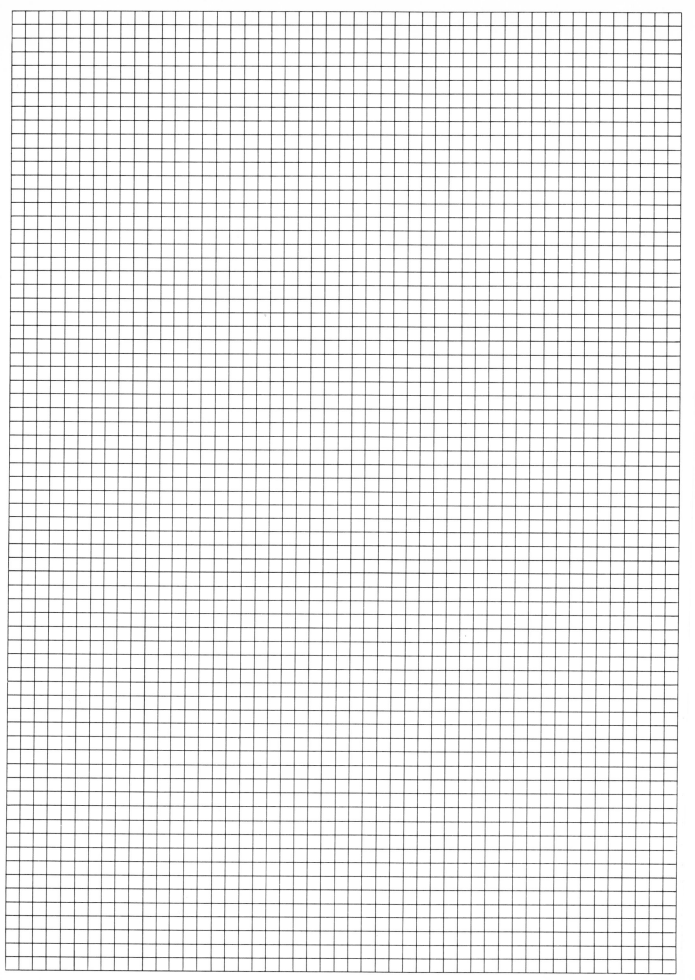

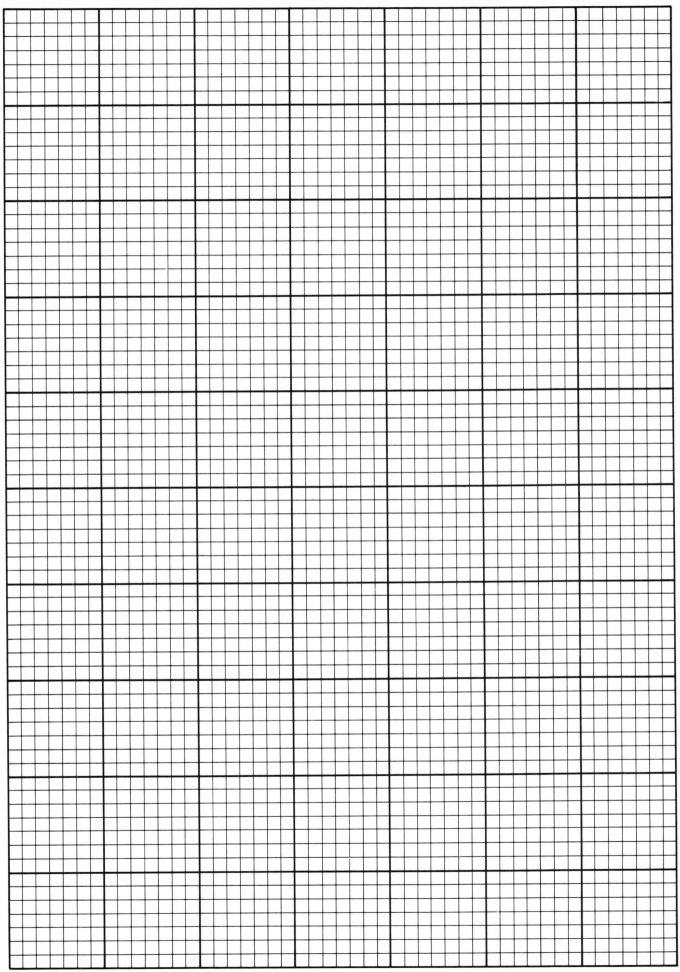

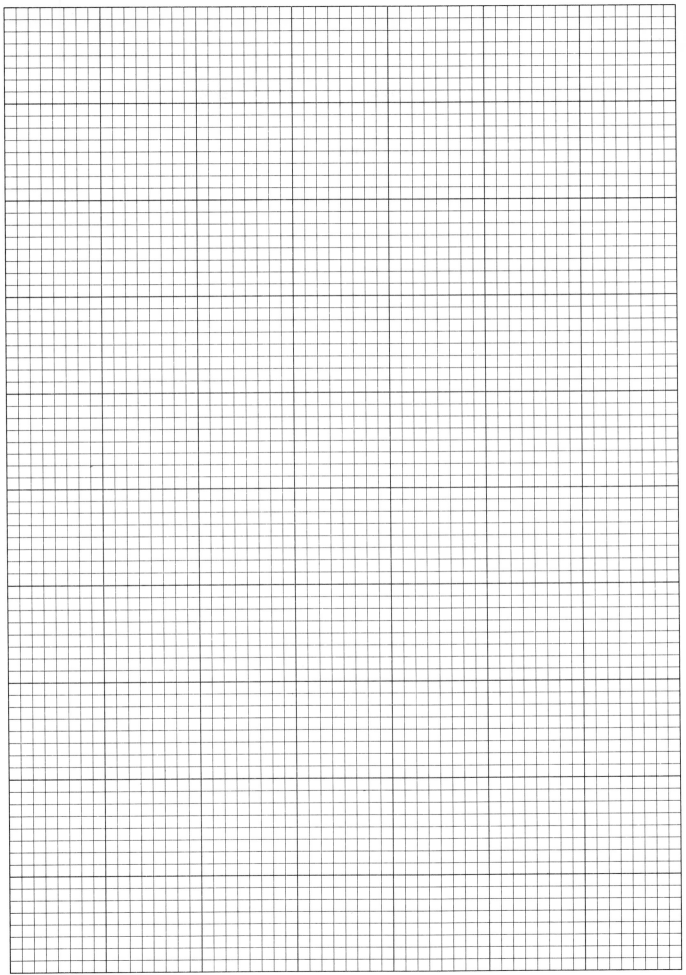

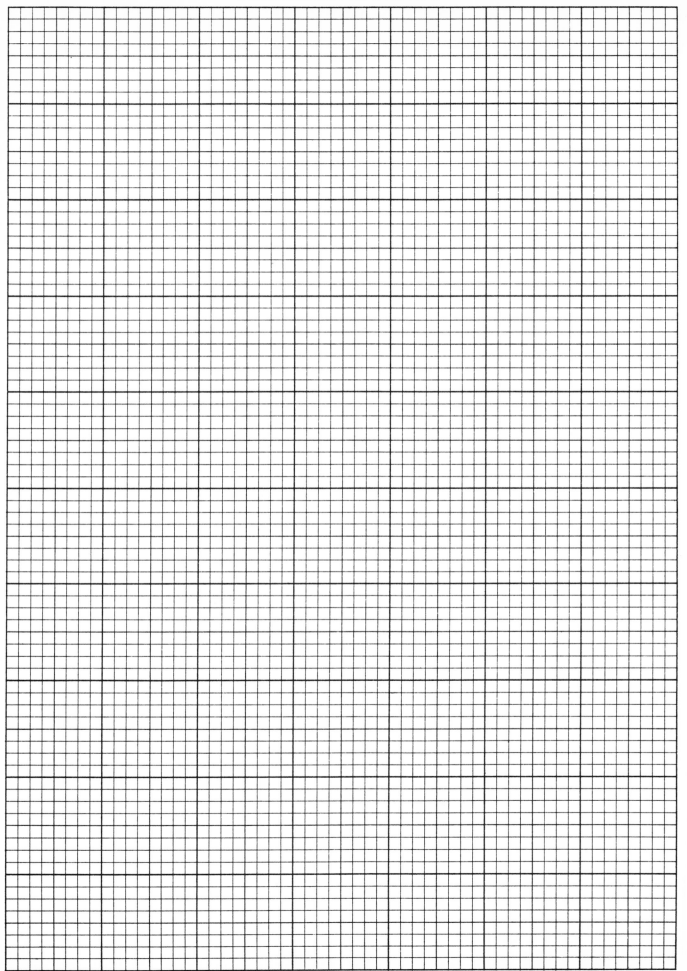

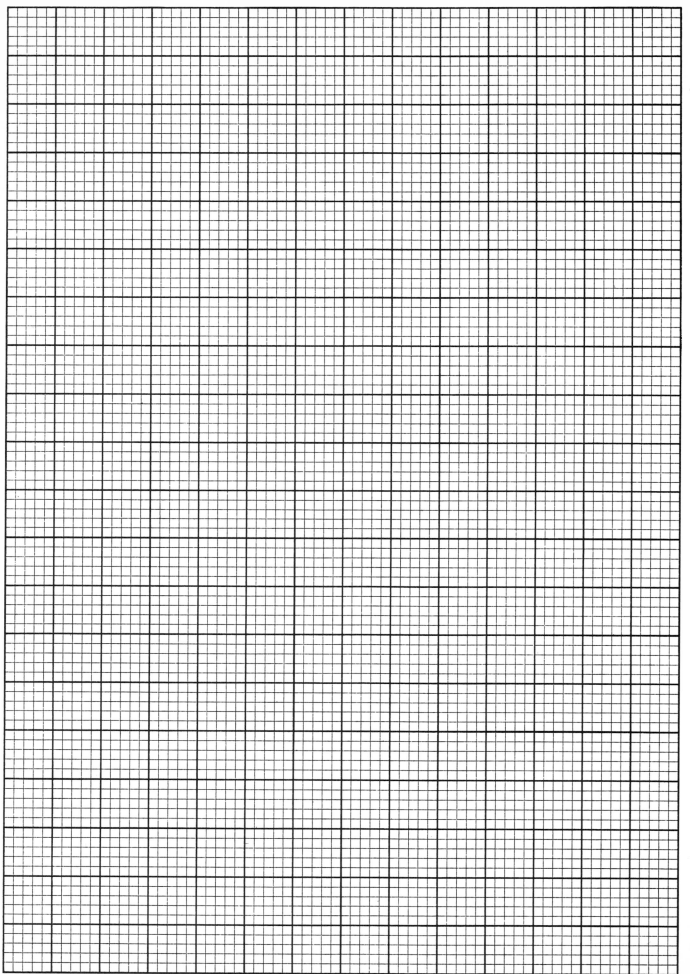

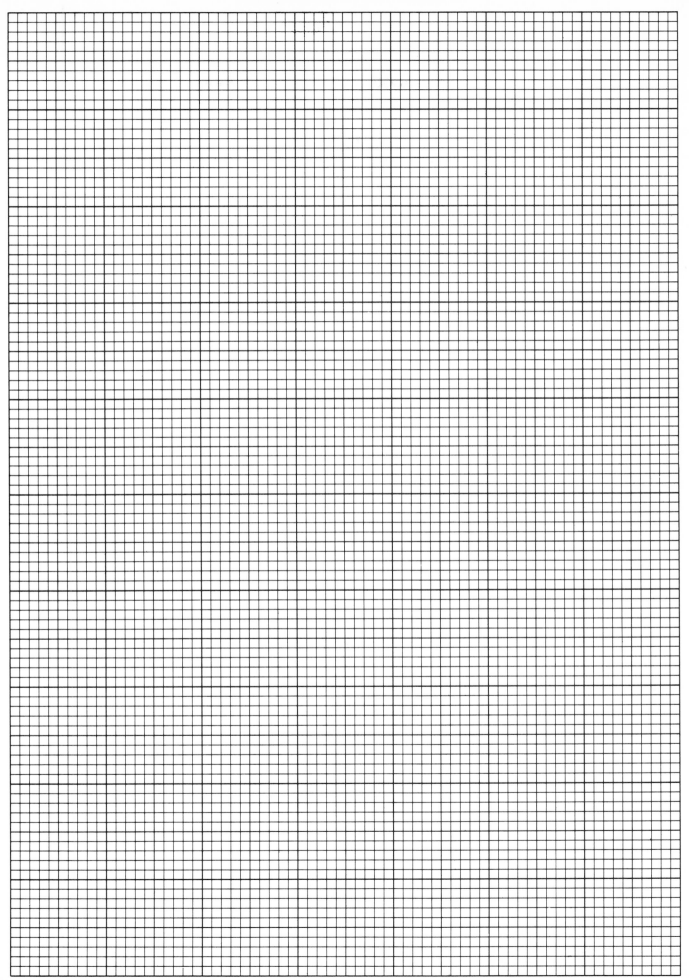

GRAPH PAPER From Your COPIER—**HPBooks**

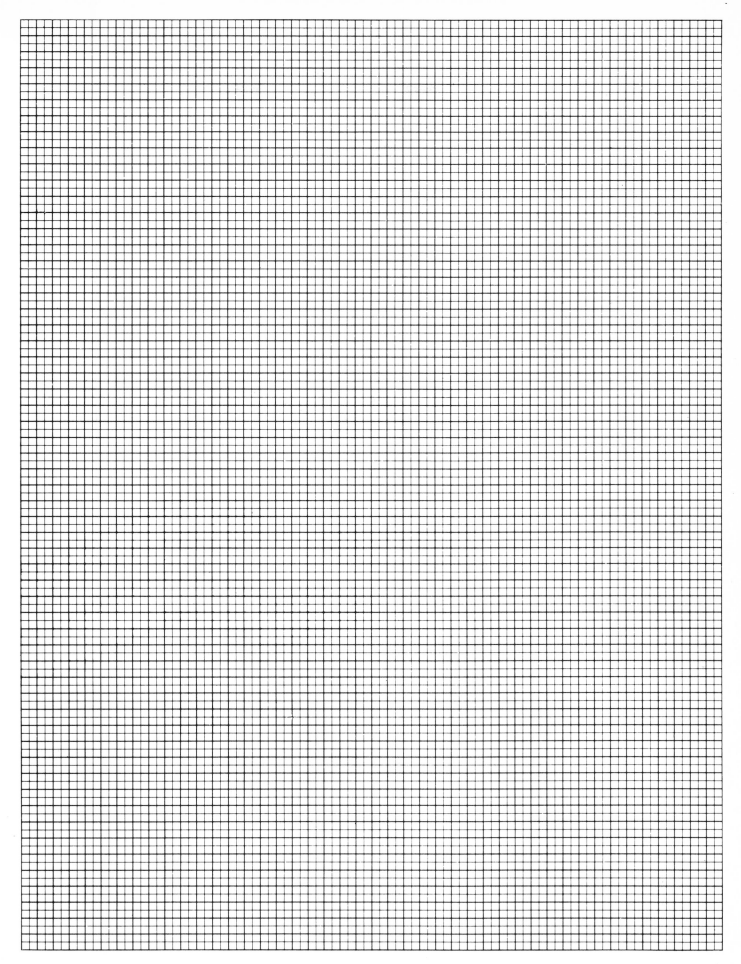

GRAPH PAPER From Your COPIER—**HPBooks**

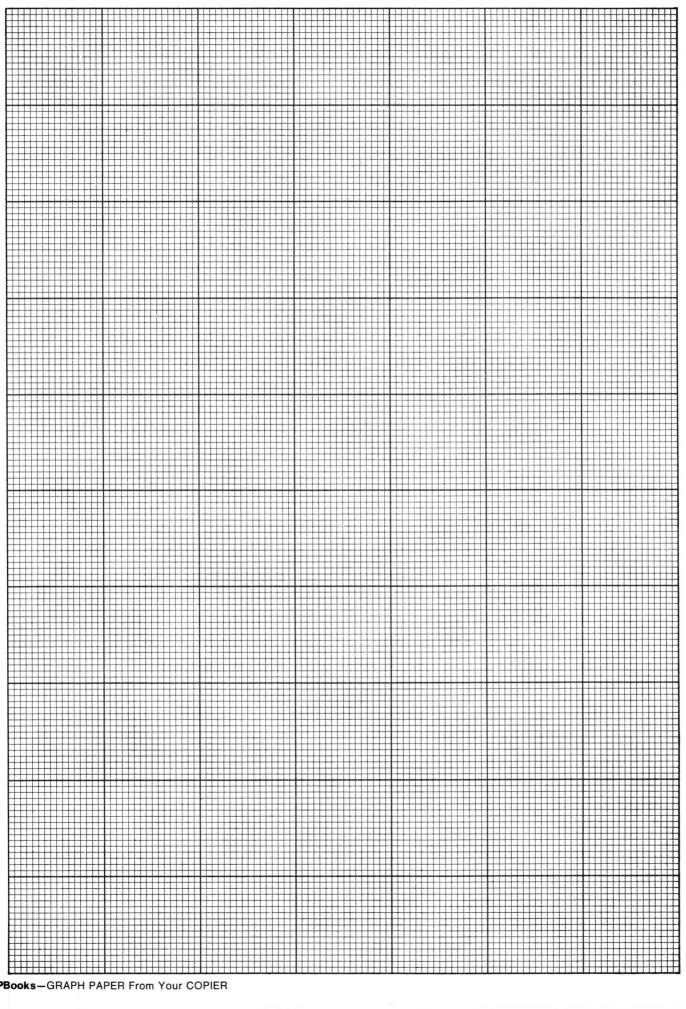

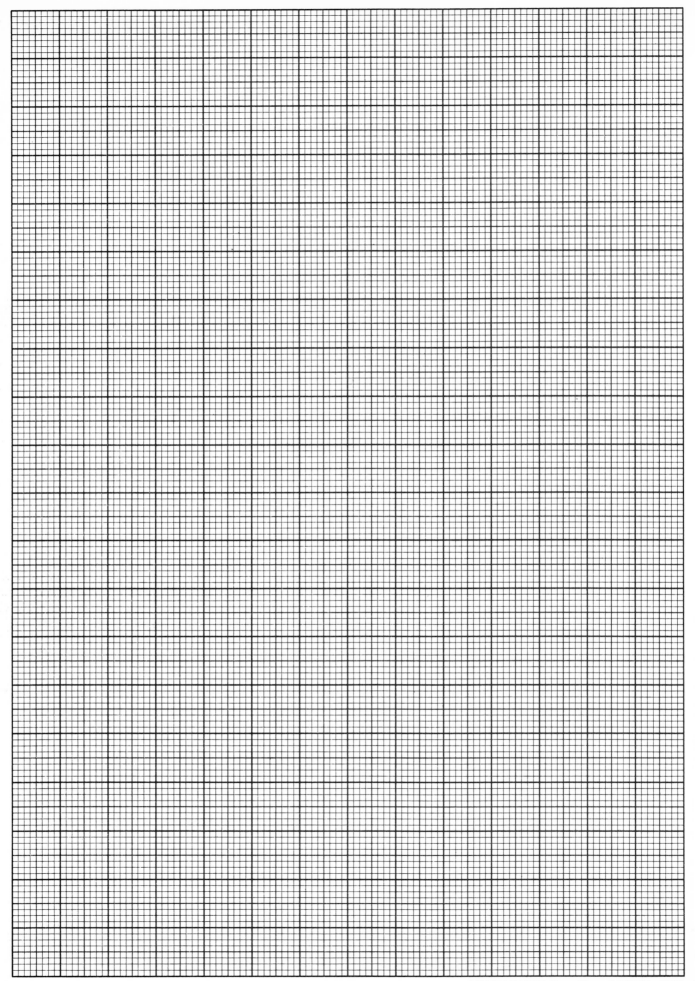

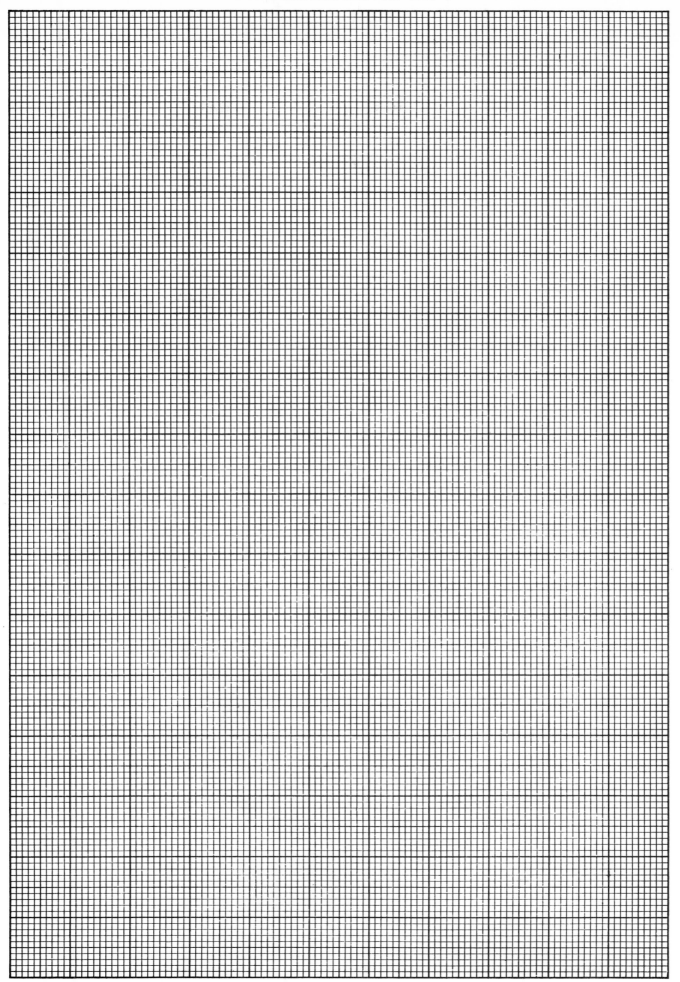

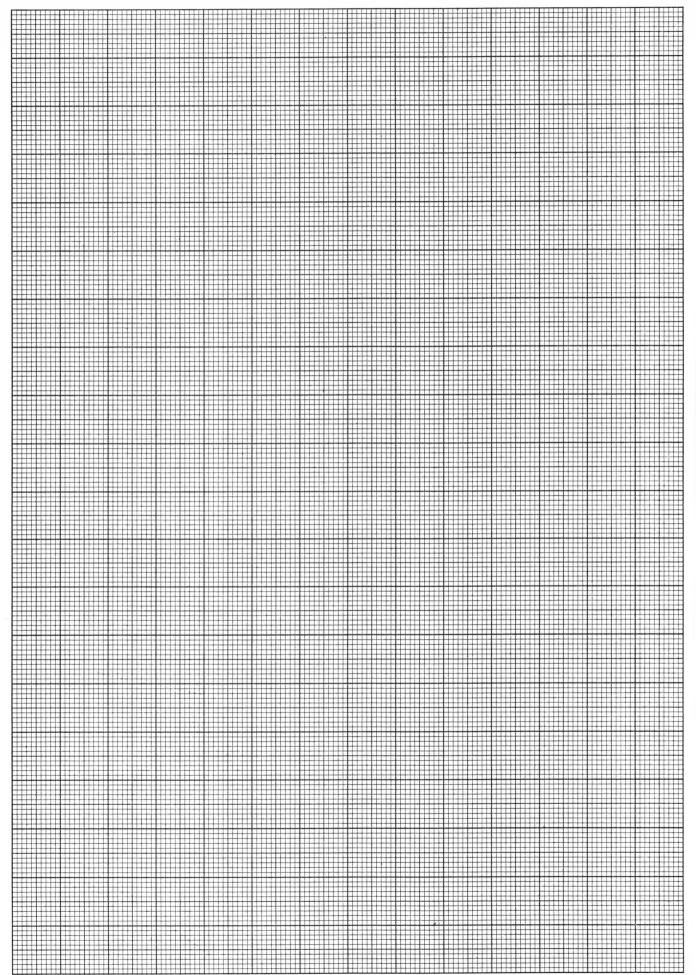

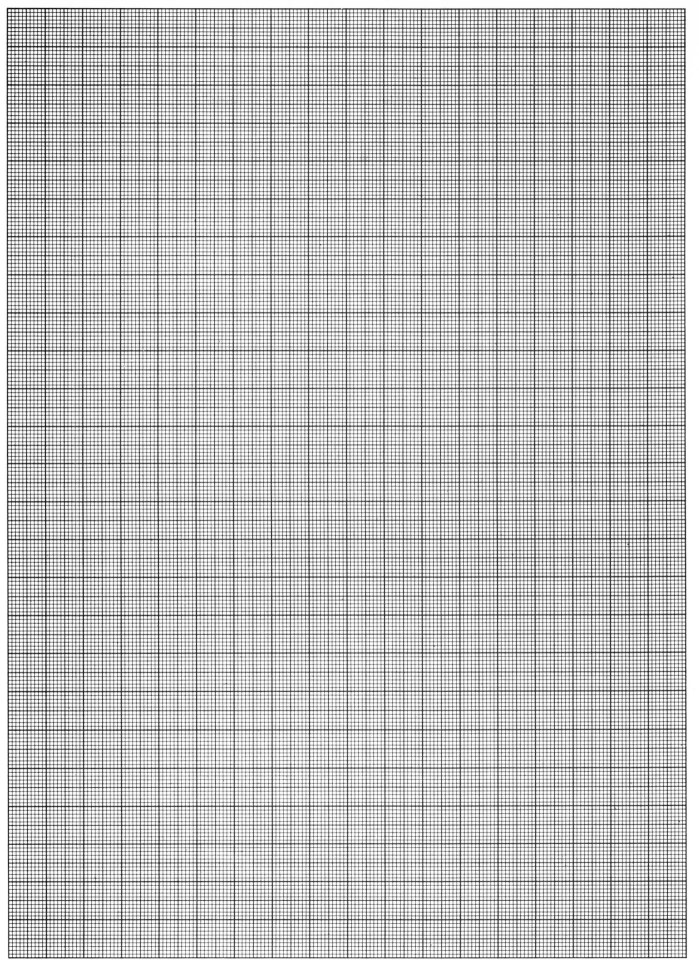

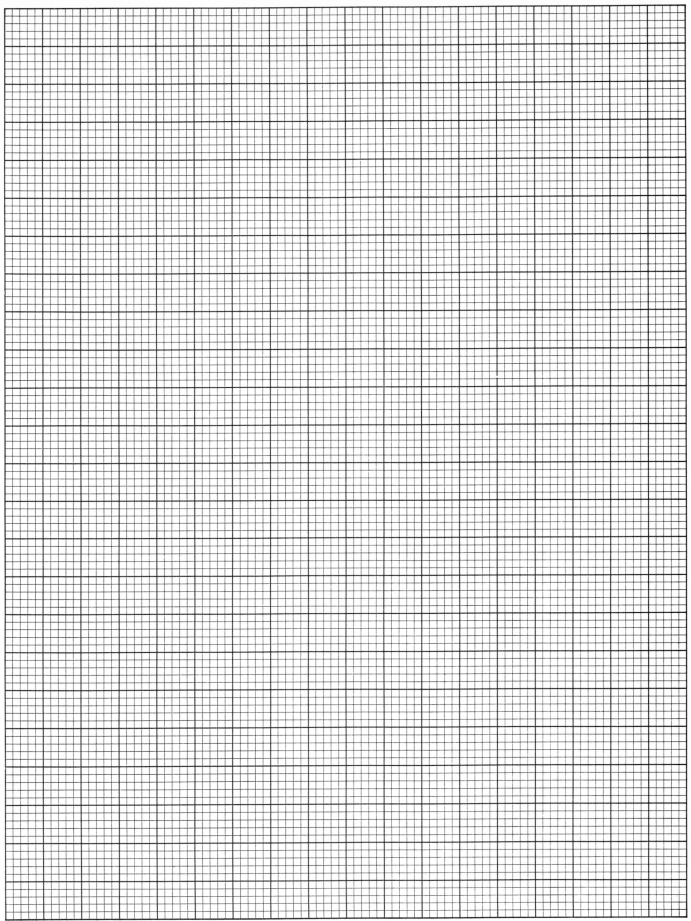

2 millimeters/Division 5th Accent

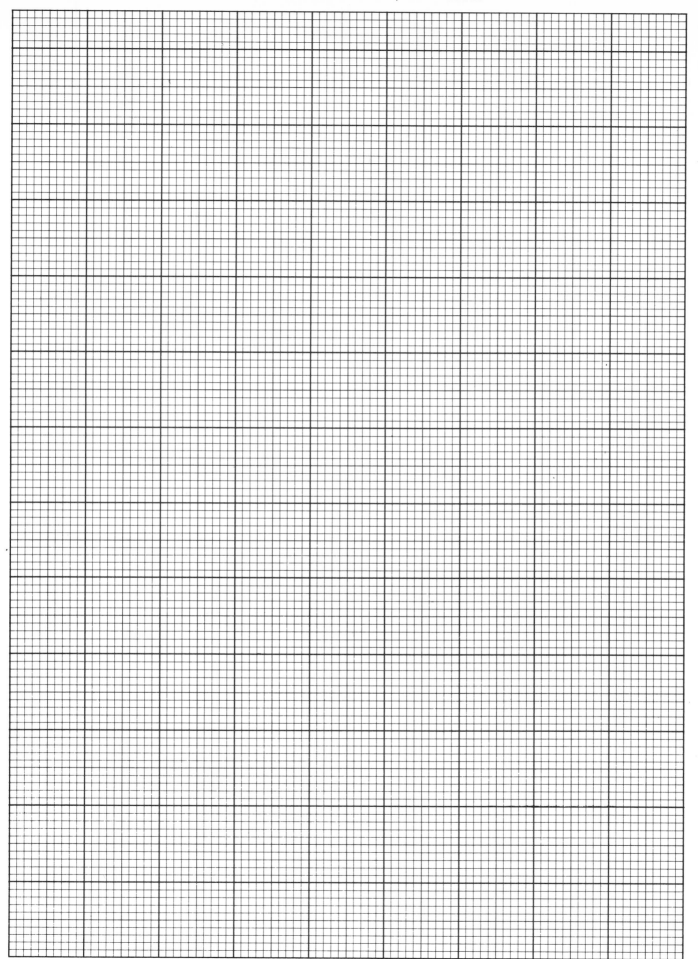

4 millimeters/Division

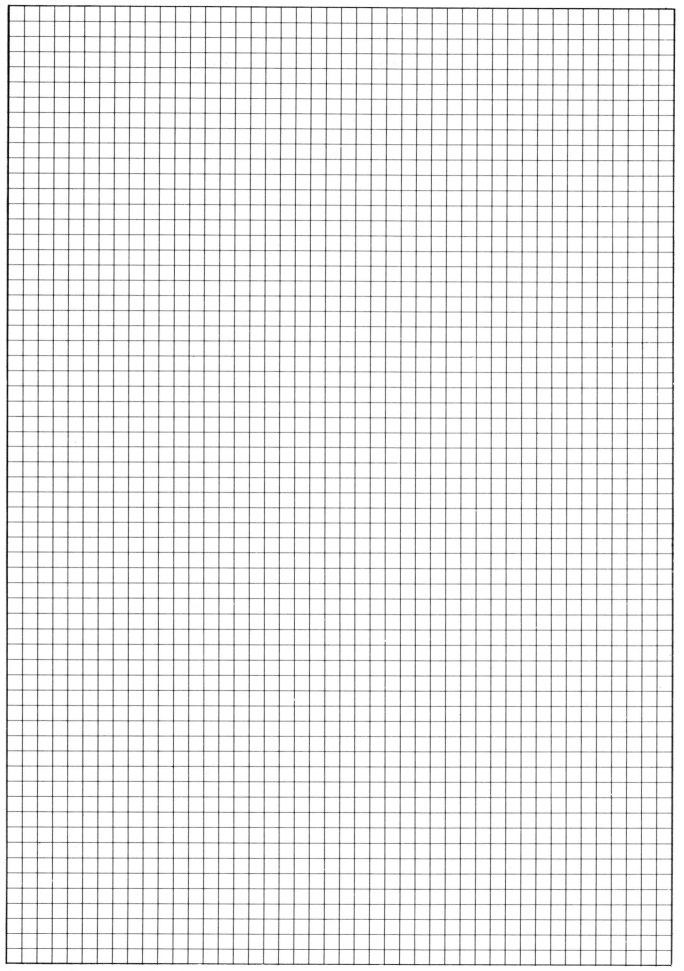

5 millimeters/Division

5 millimeters/Division 4th Accent

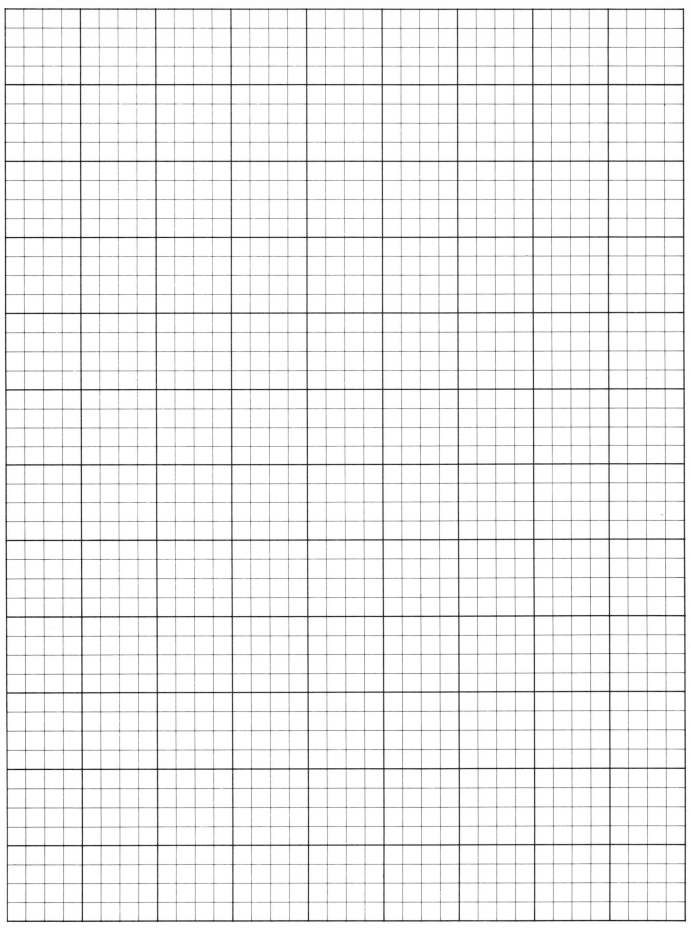

5 millimeters/Division 4th Accent

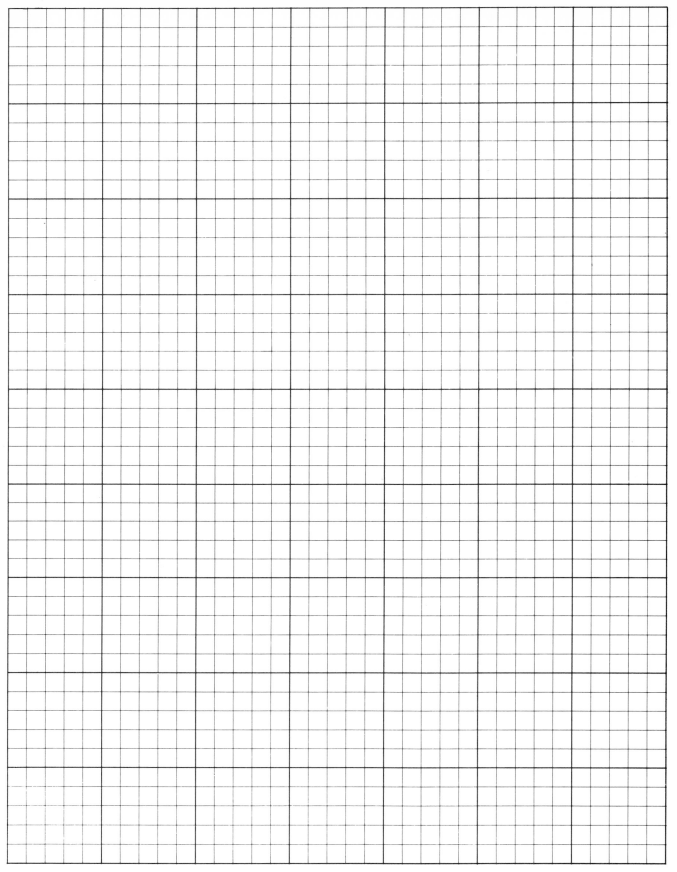

6 millimeters/Division

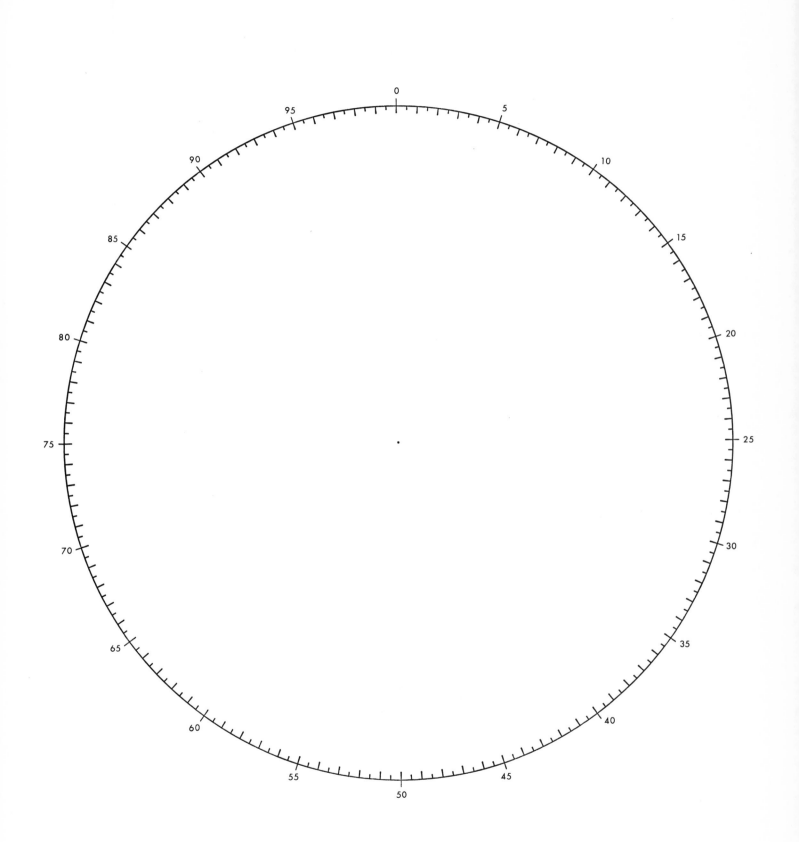

Circular Percentage 2-inch, 3-inch, 6-inch

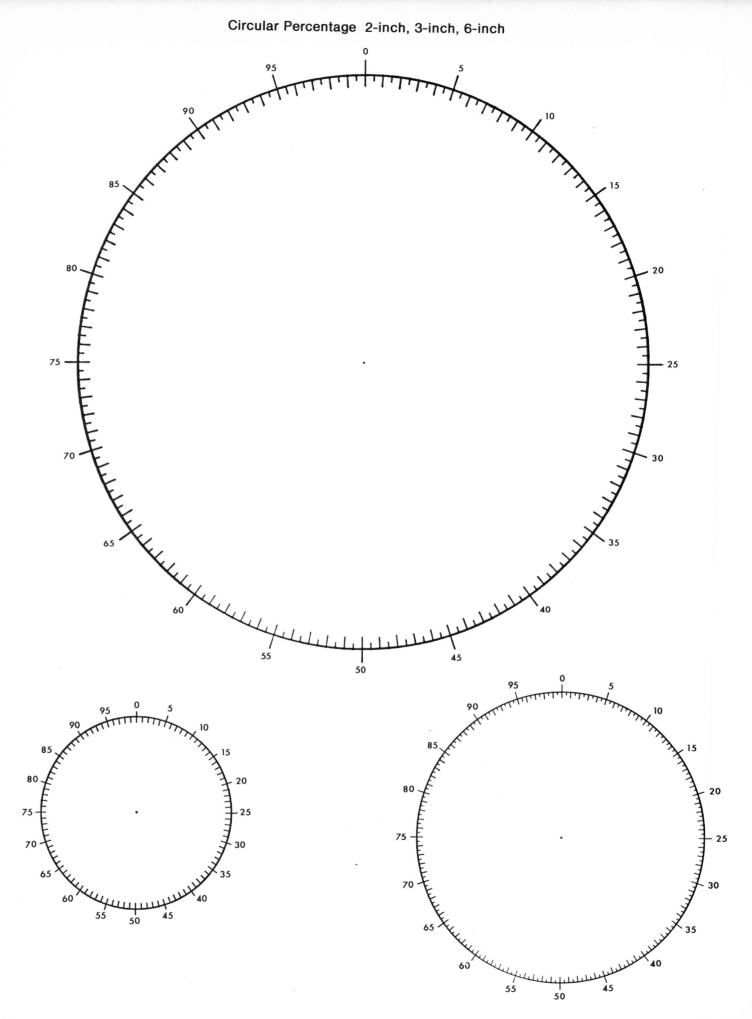

Circular Percentage 1-inch, 4-inch, 5-inch

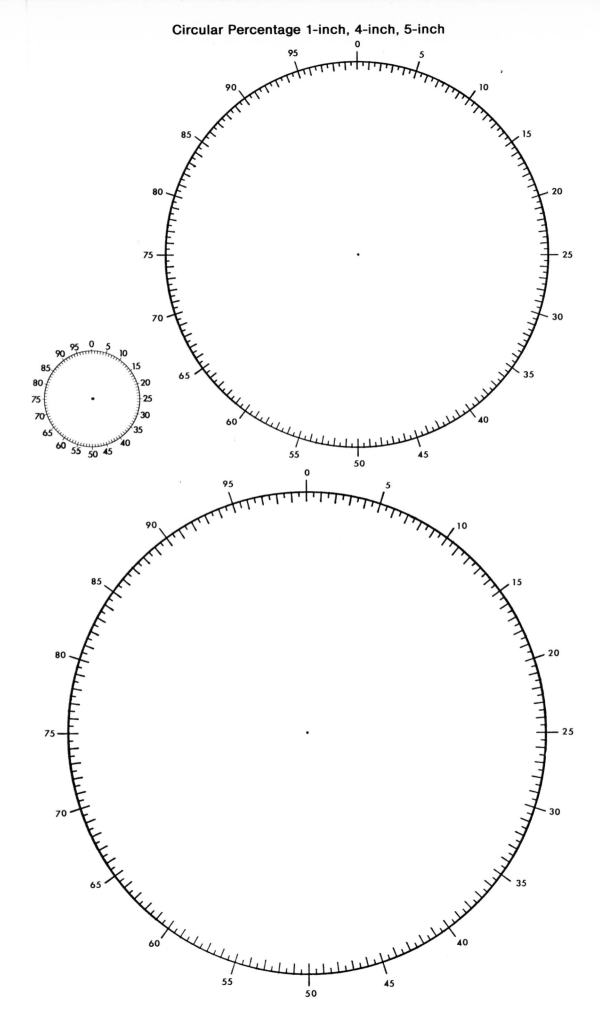

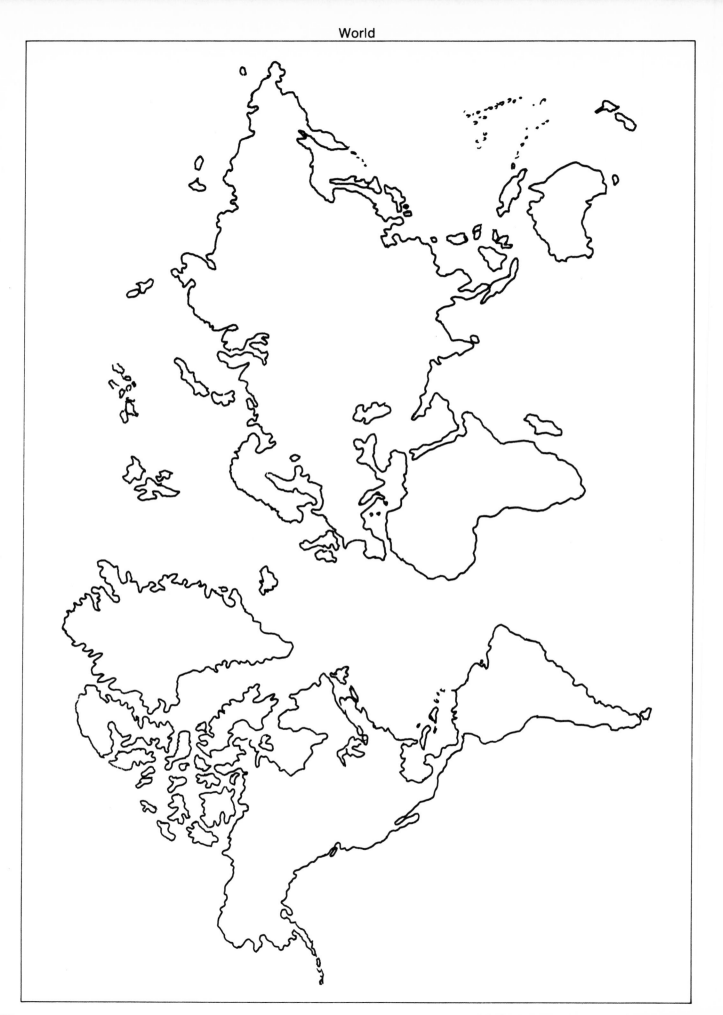

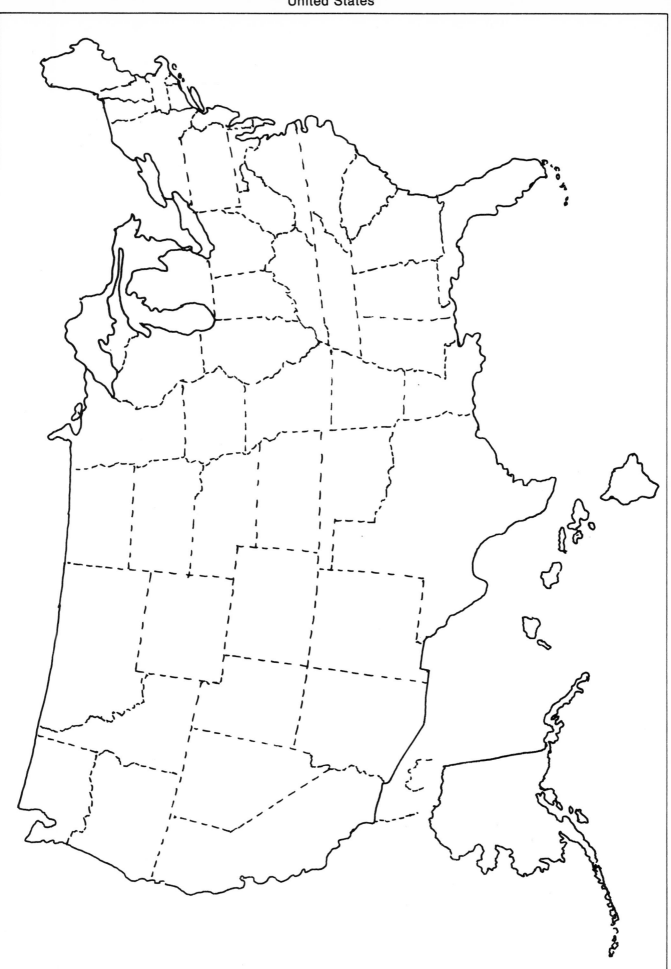

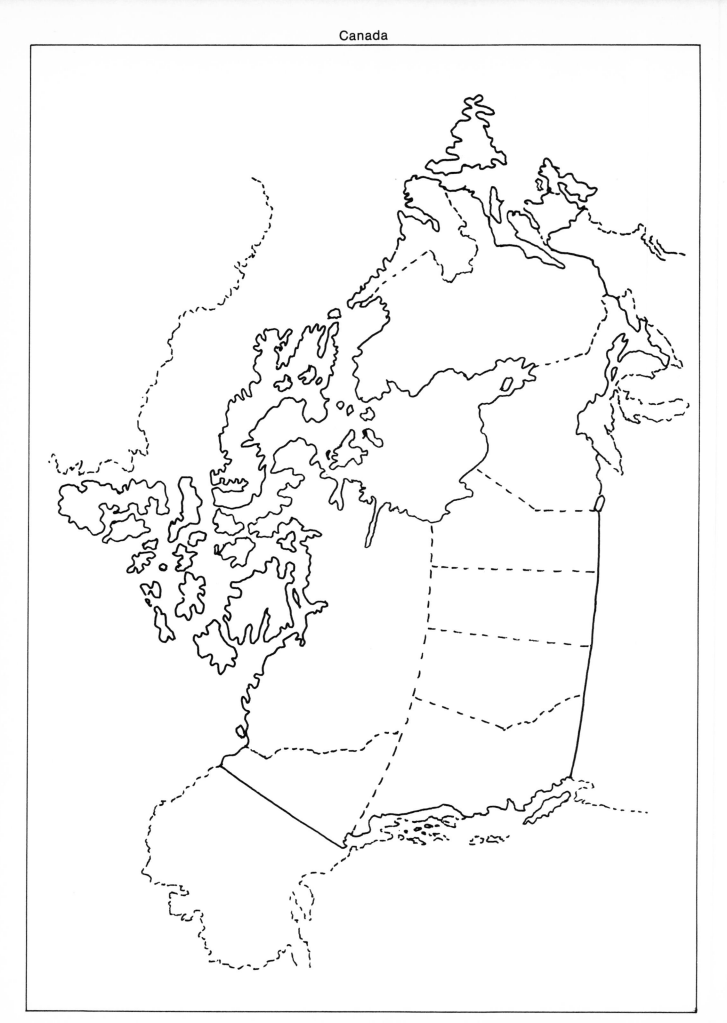

GRAPH PAPER From Your COPIER—**HPBooks**

Mexico

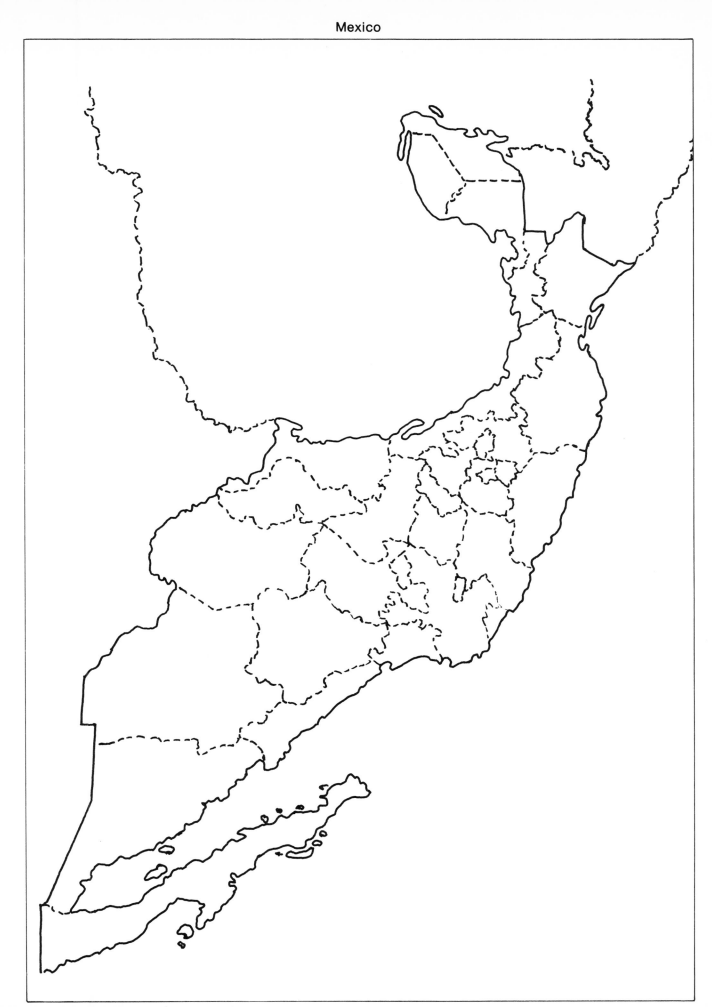

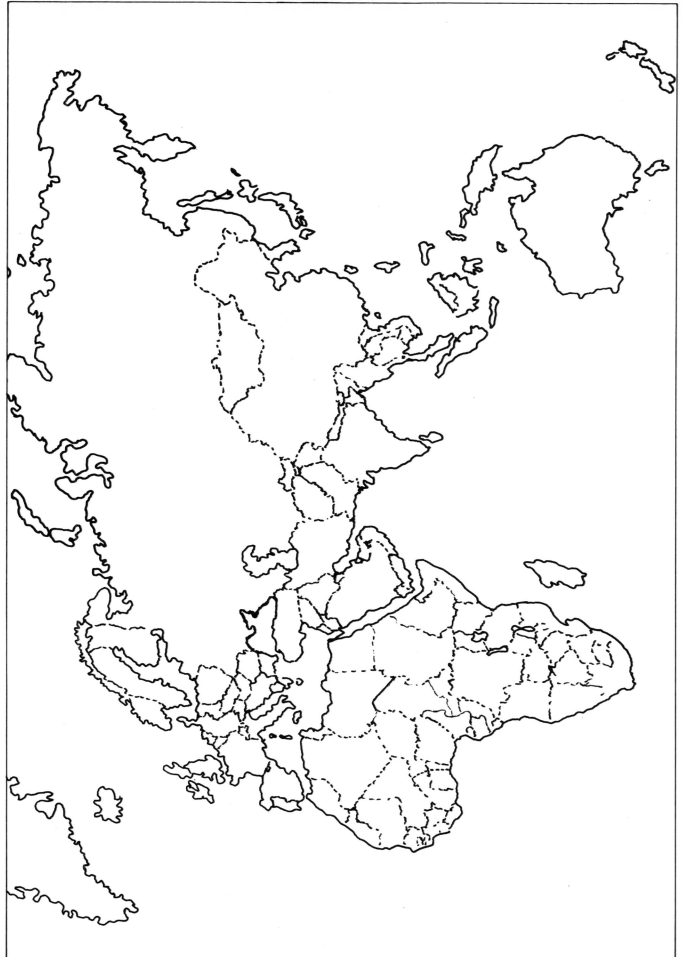

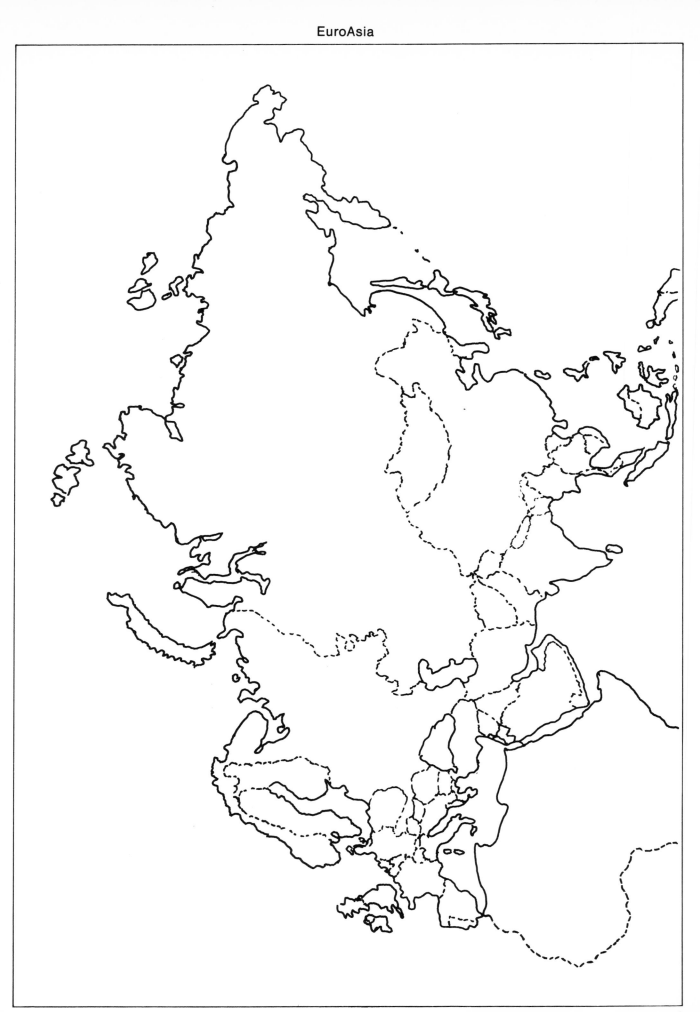

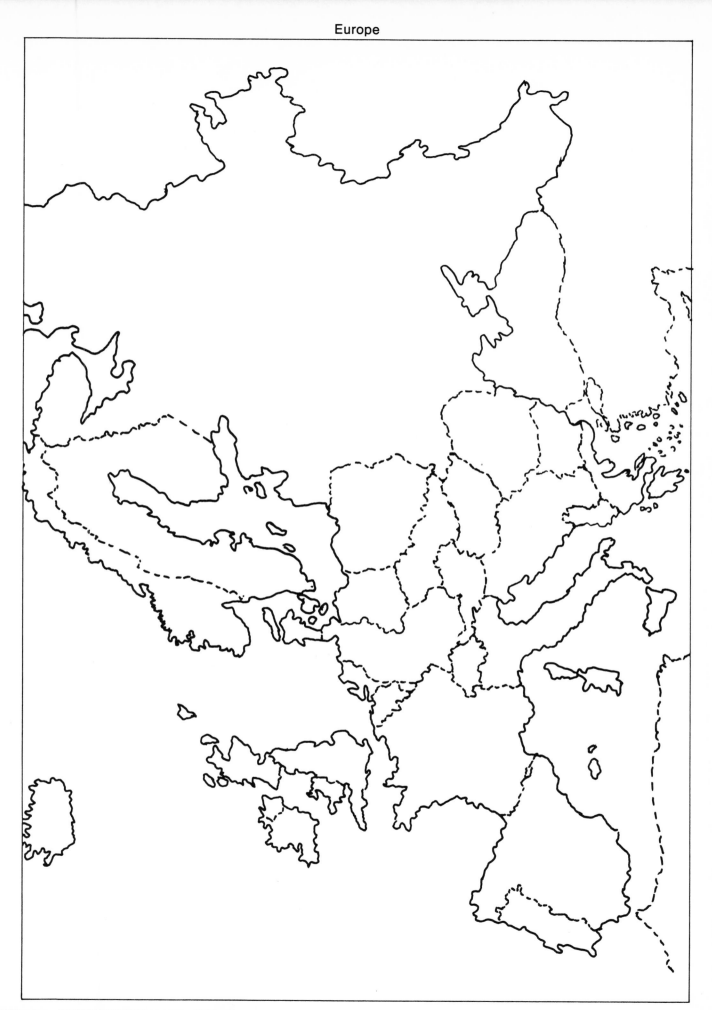

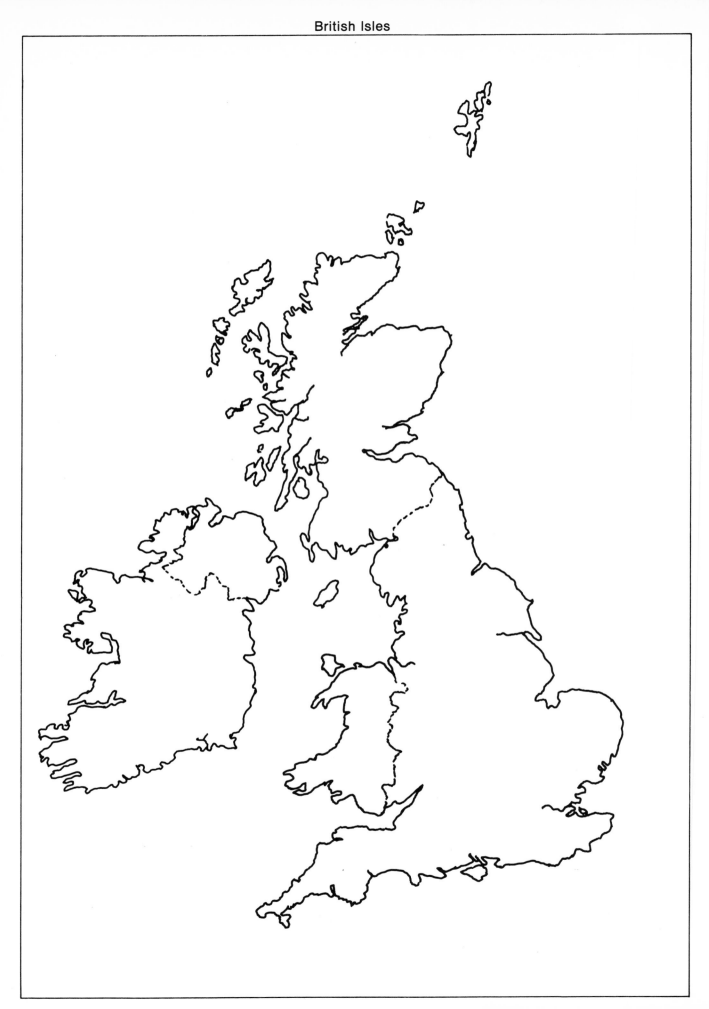

GRAPH PAPER From Your COPIER—**HPBooks**

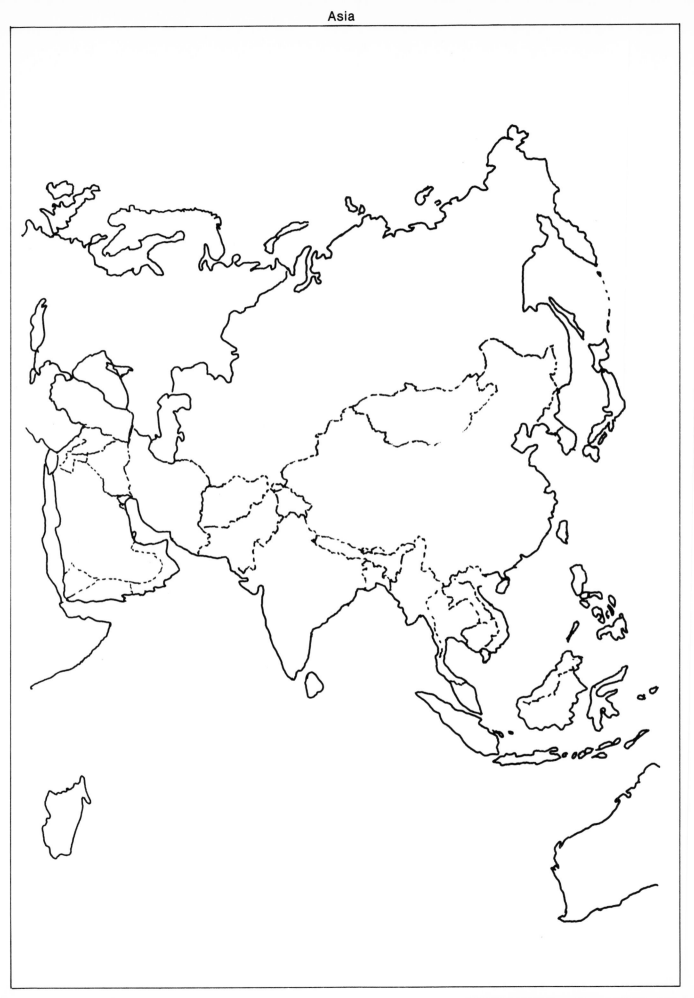

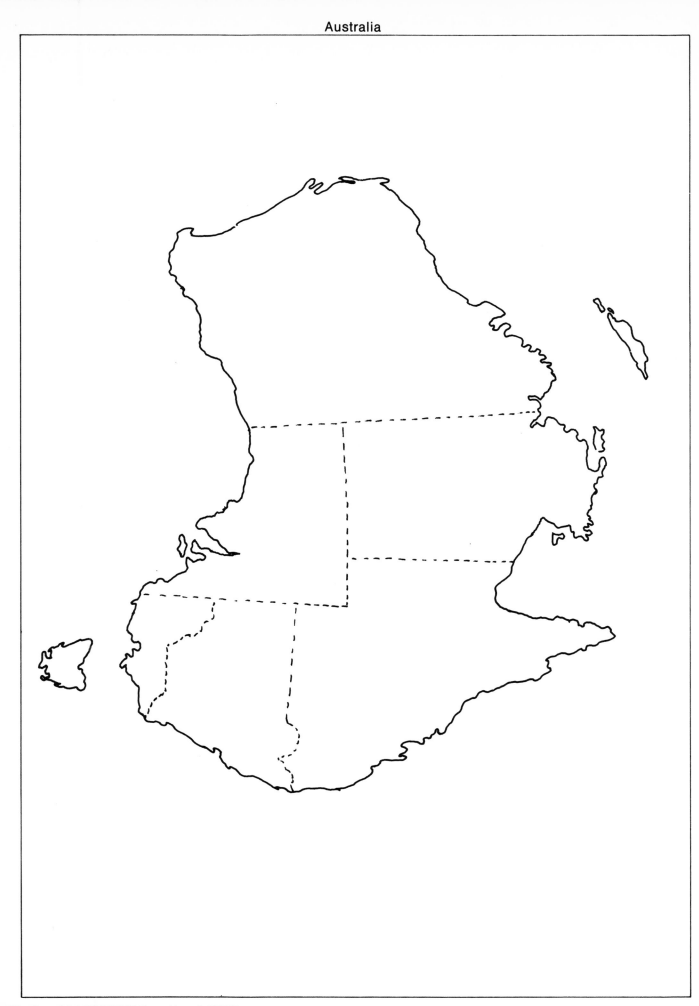

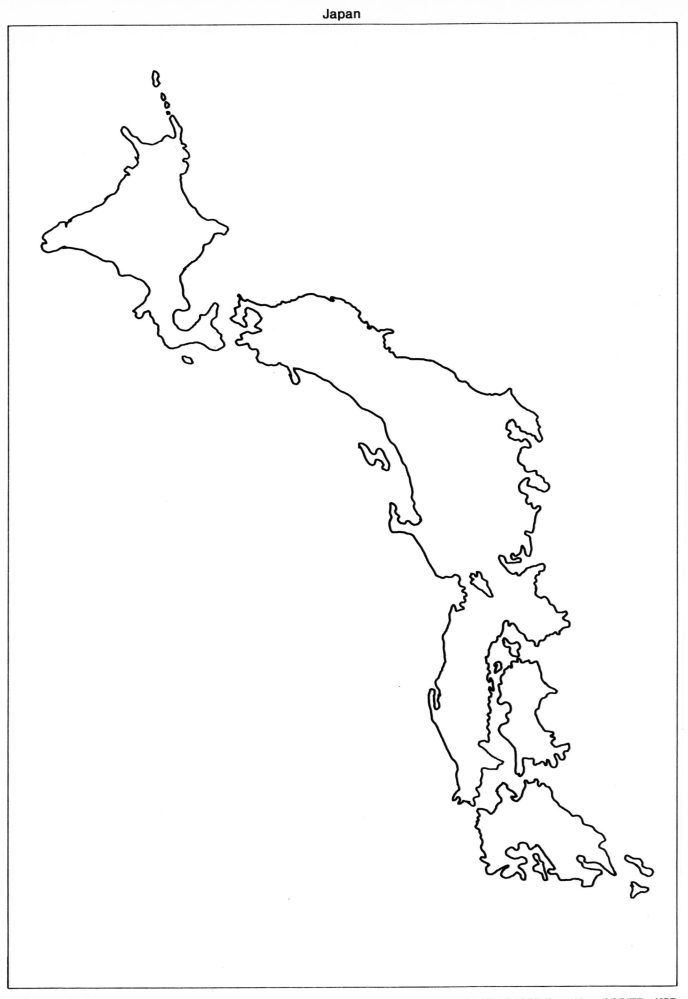

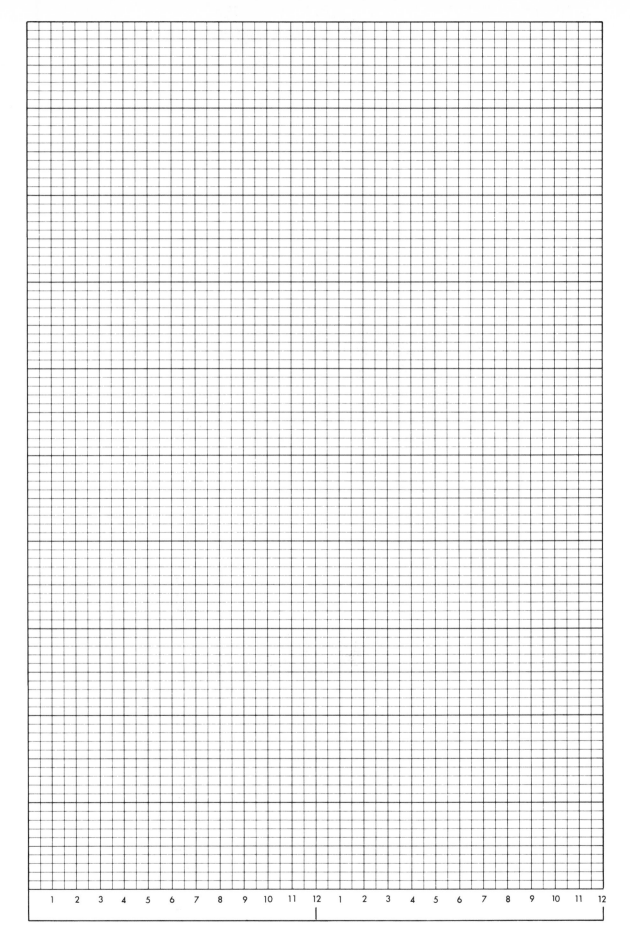

1 2 3 4 5 6 7 8 9 10 11 12 1 2 3 4 5 6 7 8 9 10 11 12

1 Month by Days 100 Divisions 5th, 10th Accent

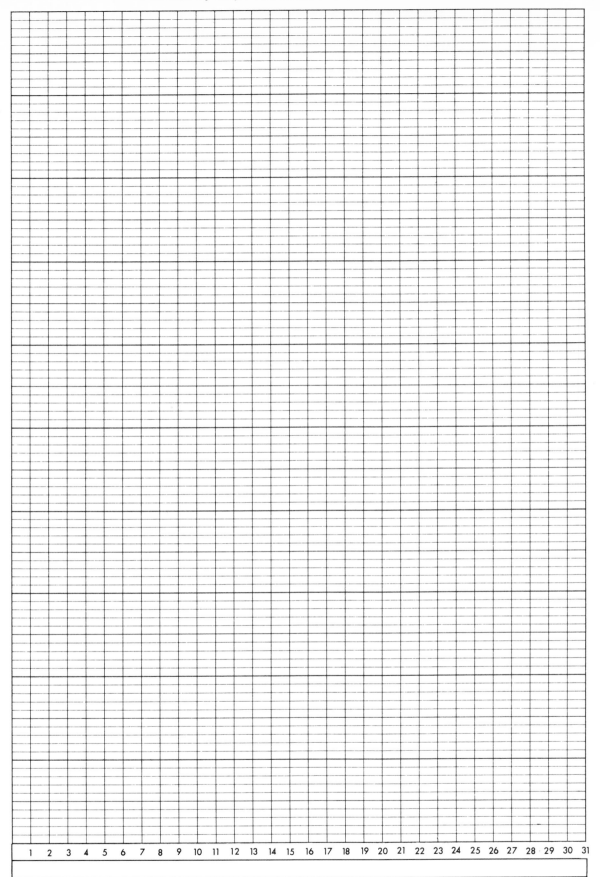

1 2 3 4 5 6 7 8 9 10 11 12 13 14 15 16 17 18 19 20 21 22 23 24 25 26 27 28 29 30 31

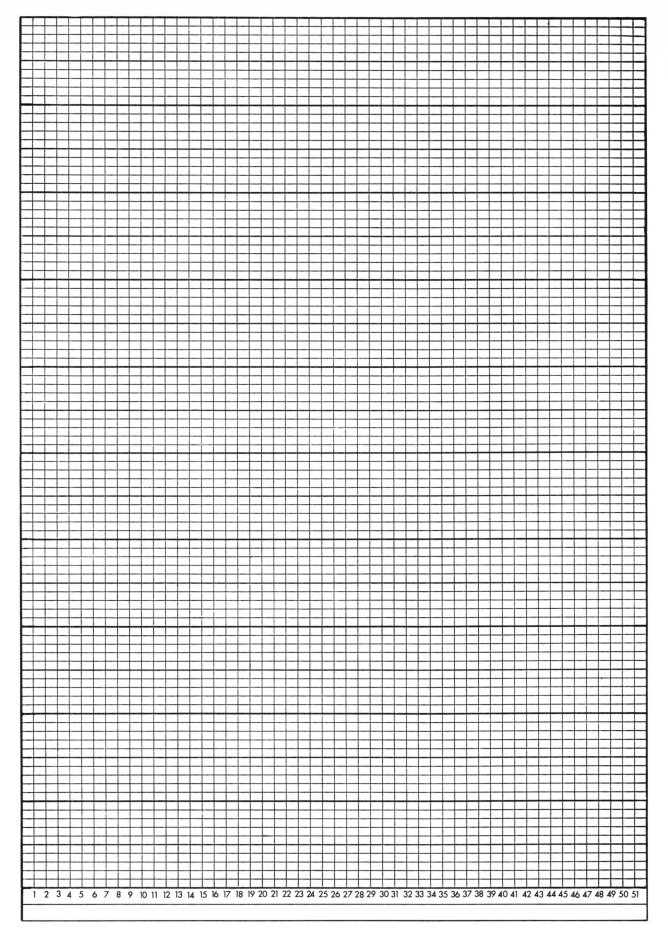

1 2 3 4 5 6 7 8 9 10 11 12 13 14 15 16 17 18 19 20 21 22 23 24 25 26 27 28 29 30 31 32 33 34 35 36 37 38 39 40 41 42 43 44 45 46 47 48 49 50 51

1 Year by Months 120 Divisions 10th Accent

3 Years by Months 100 Divisions 5th, 10th Accent

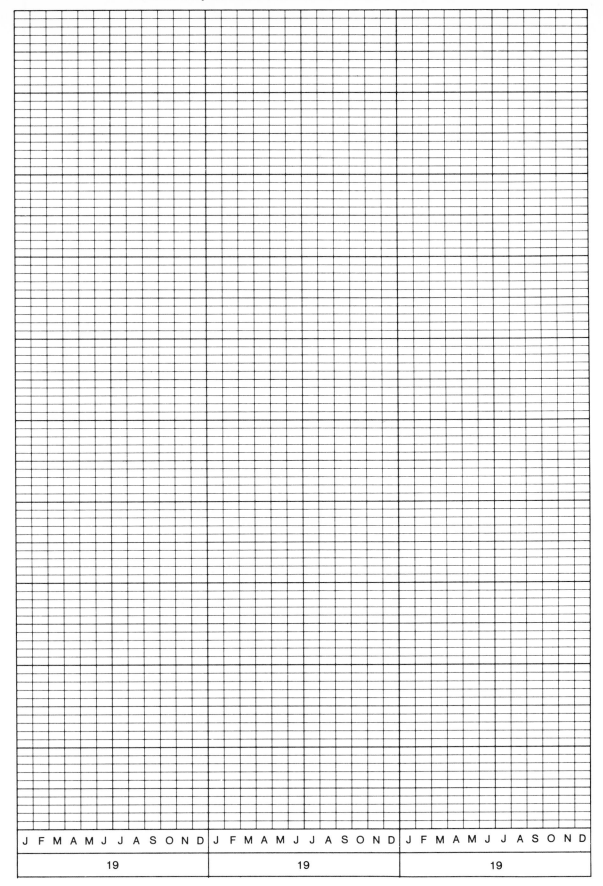

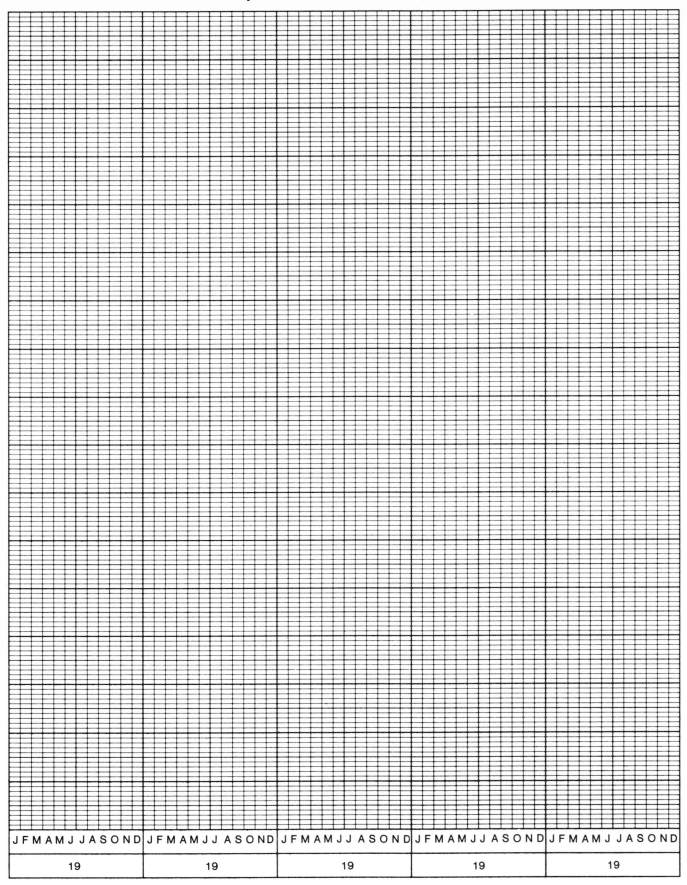

J F M A M J J A S O N D J F M A M J J A S O N D J F M A M J J A S O N D J F M A M J J A S O N D J F M A M J J A S O N D

19   19   19   19   19

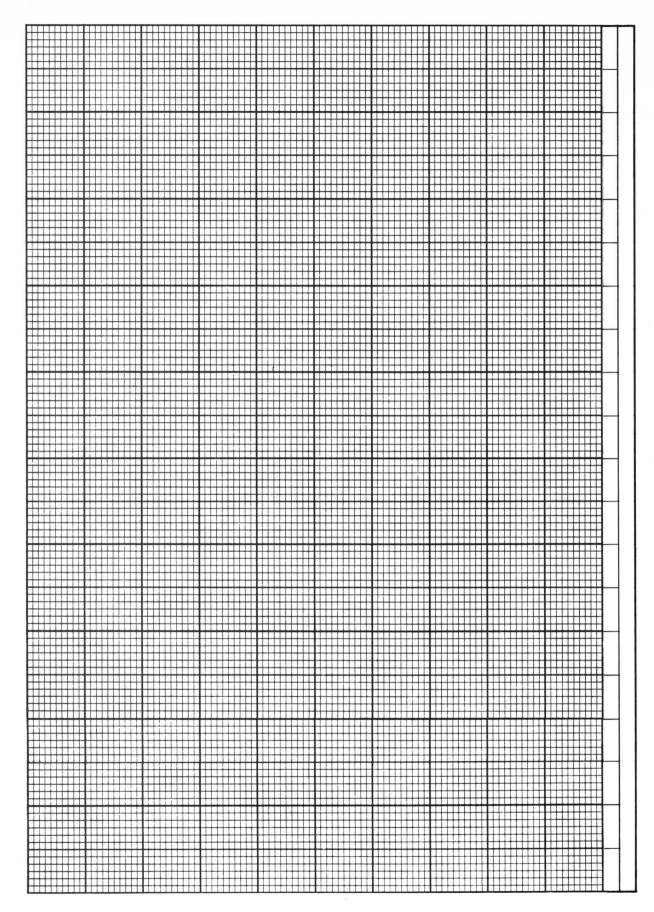

27 Weeks by 5 Days (Stock Market) 25-Point 1/8 Point/Division

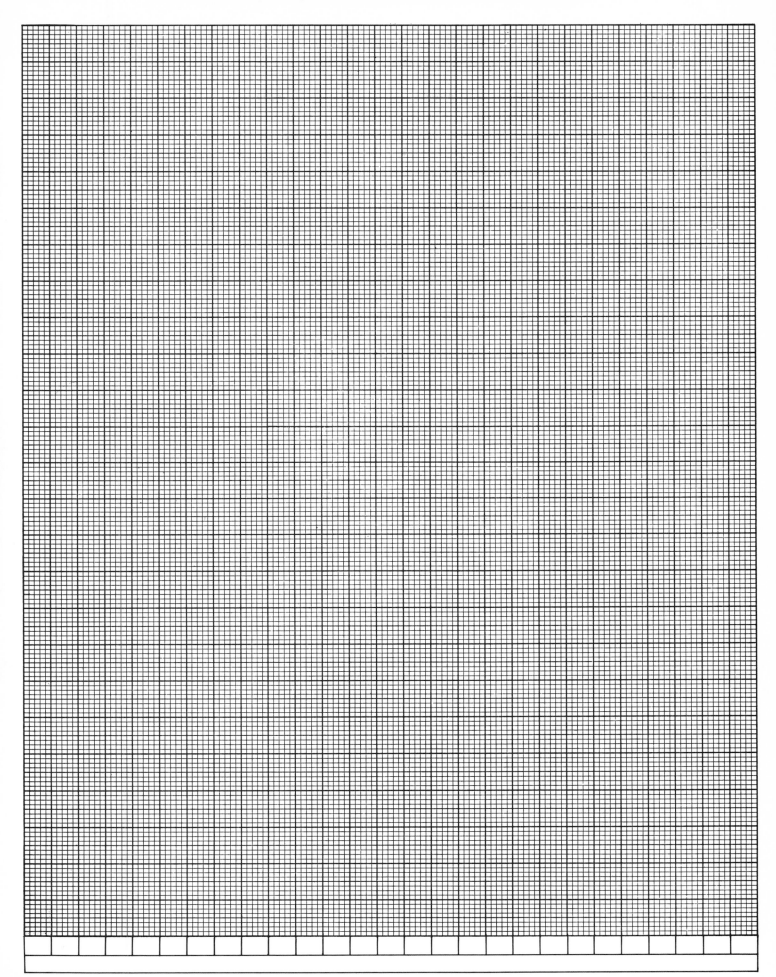

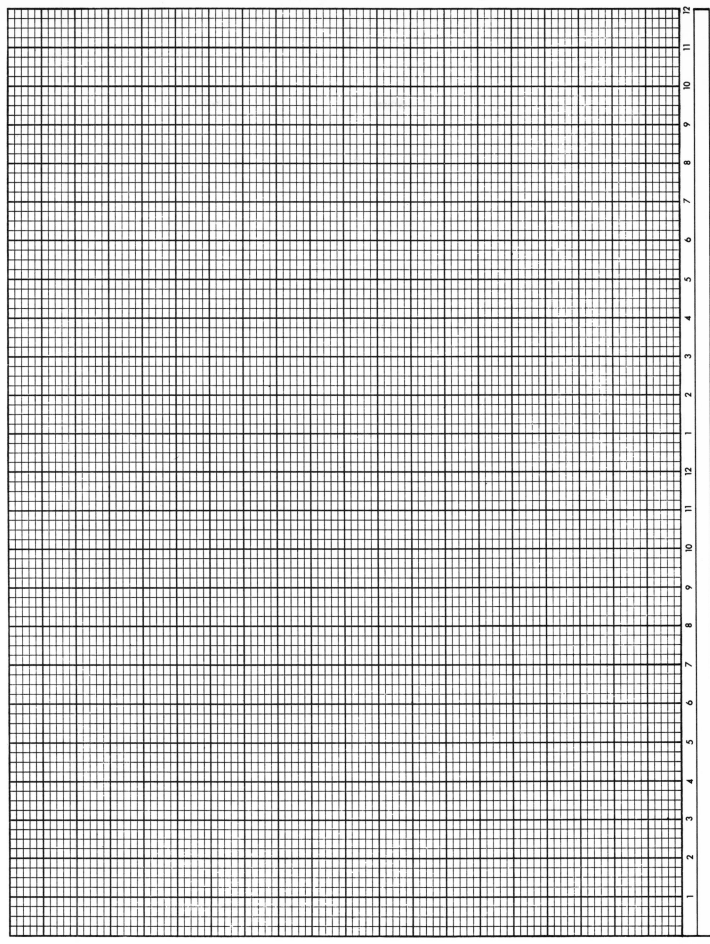

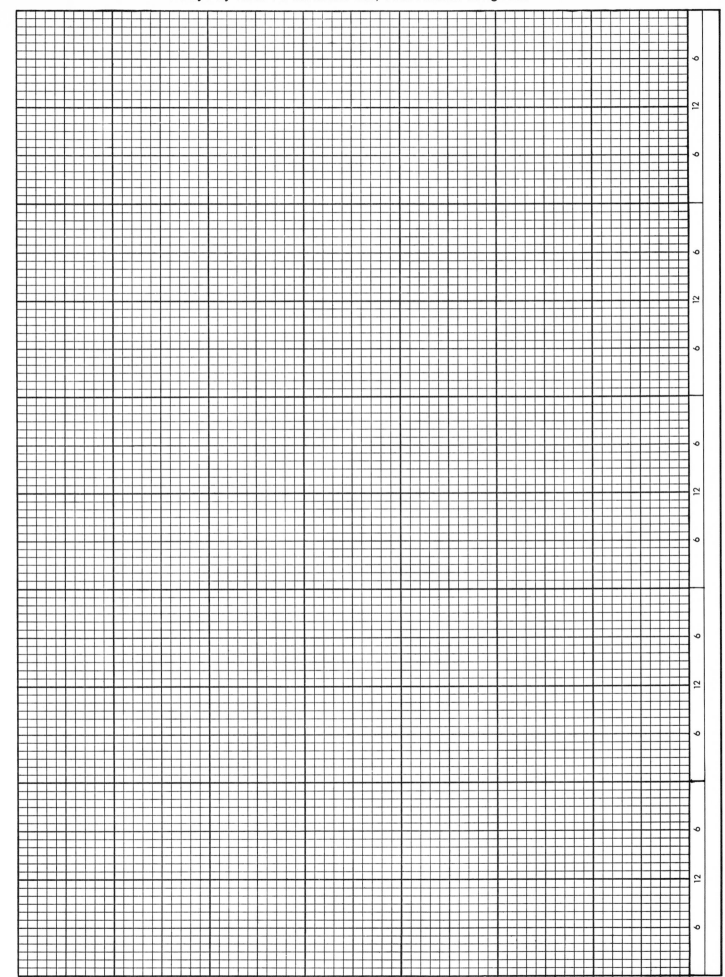

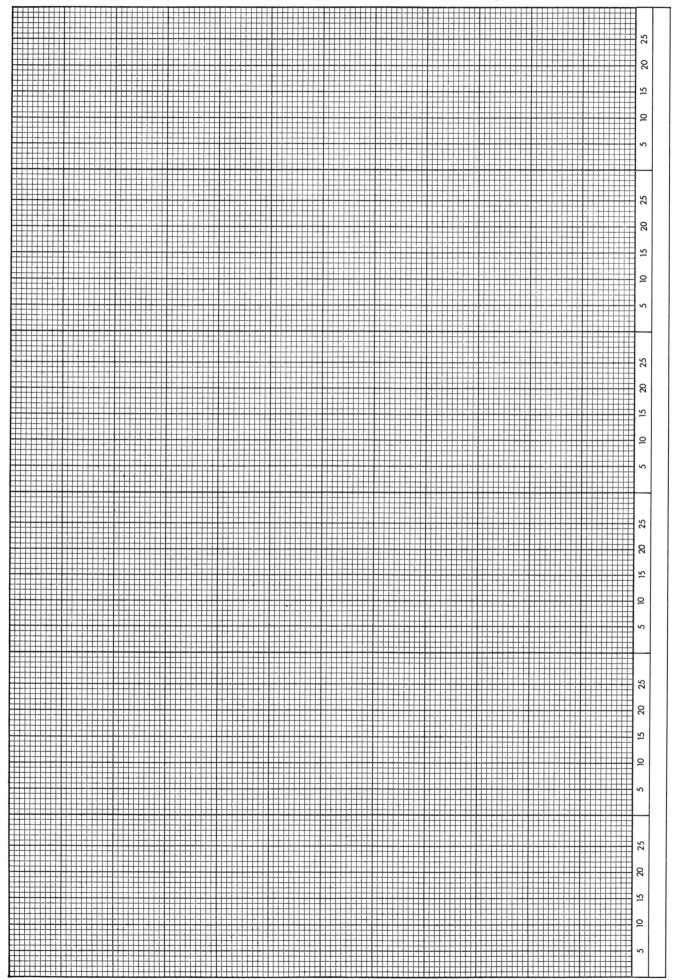

1 Year by Months 100 Divisions 5th, 10th Accent Long Axis

19

| JAN | FEB | MAR | APR | MAY | JUNE | JULY | AUG | SEPT | OCT | NOV | DEC |

5 Years by Months 100 Divisions 5th, 10th Accent Long Axis

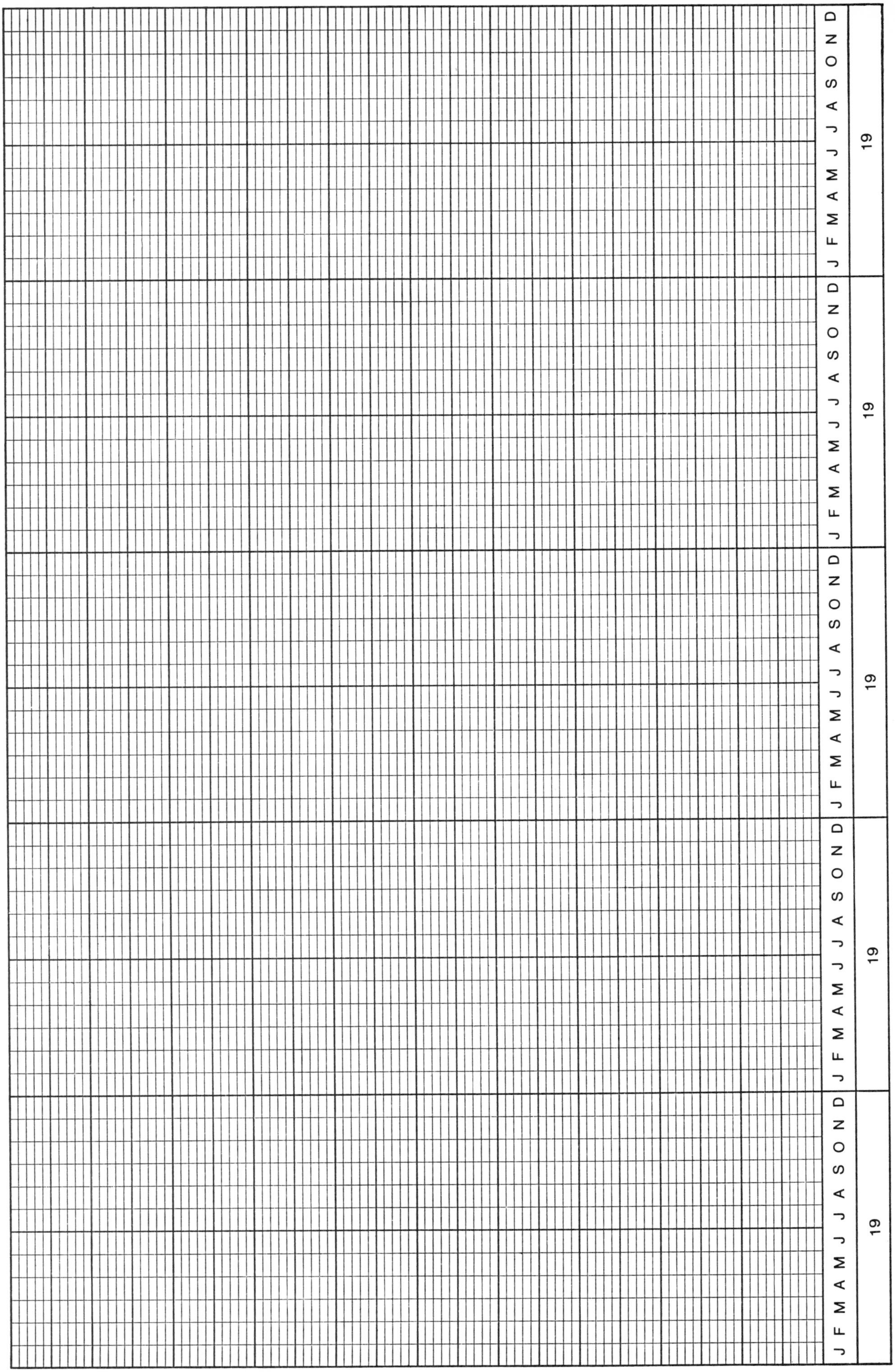

J F M A M J J A S O N D   19

J F M A M J J A S O N D   19

J F M A M J J A S O N D   19

J F M A M J J A S O N D   19

J F M A M J J A S O N D   19

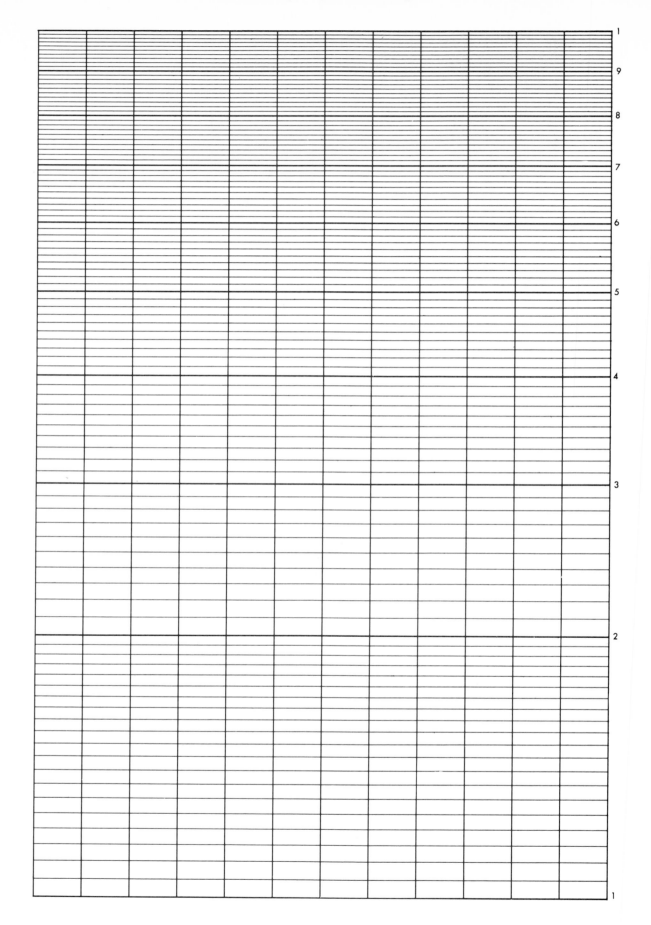

12 Divisions 3rd Accent by 2 Cycle Semi-Log

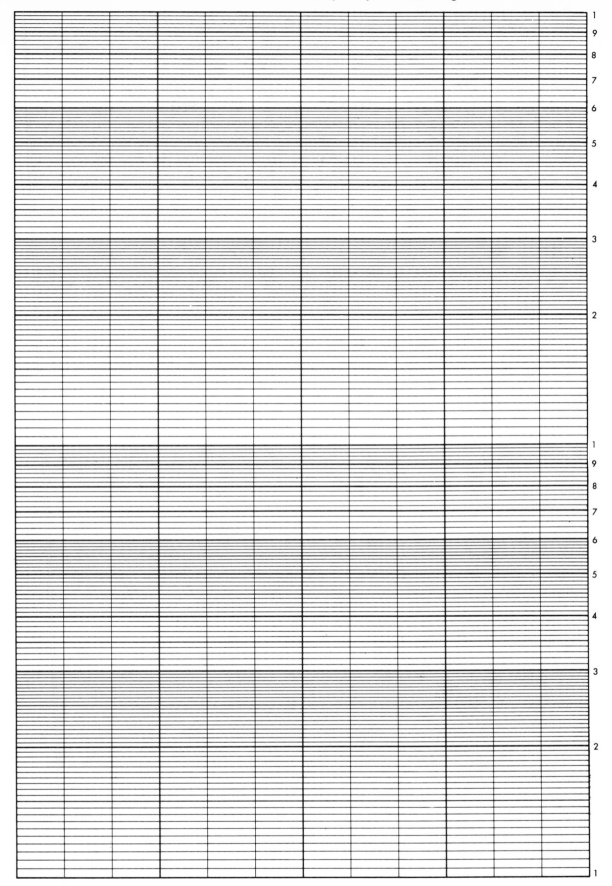

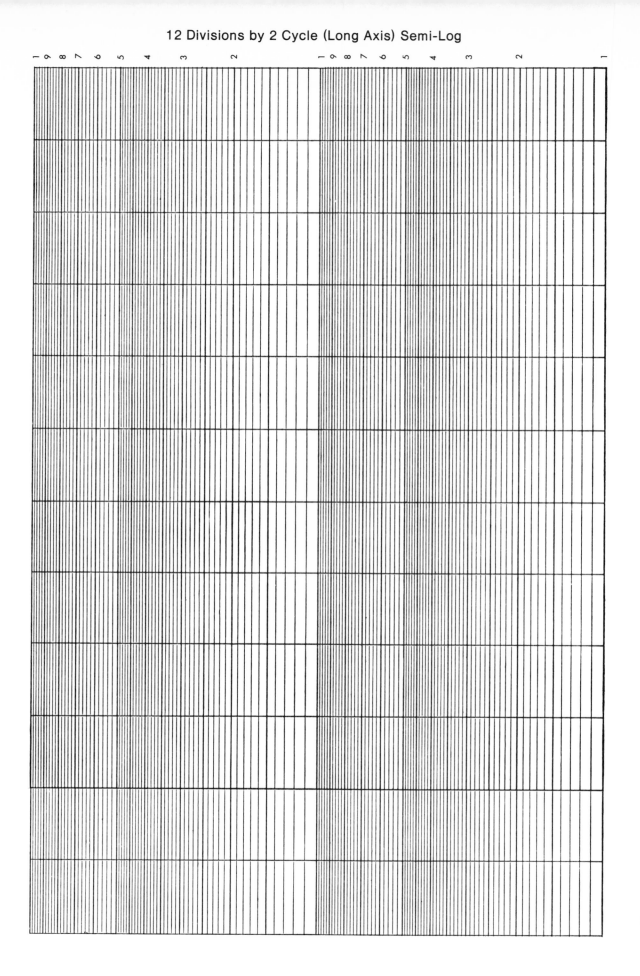

12 Divisions by 3 Cycle Semi-Log

31 Divisions by 2 Cycle Semi-Log

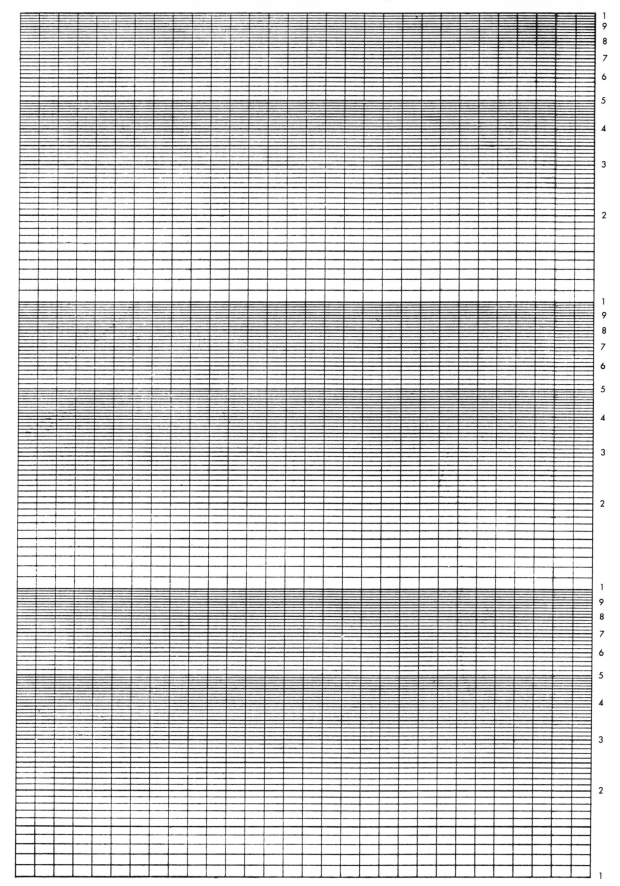

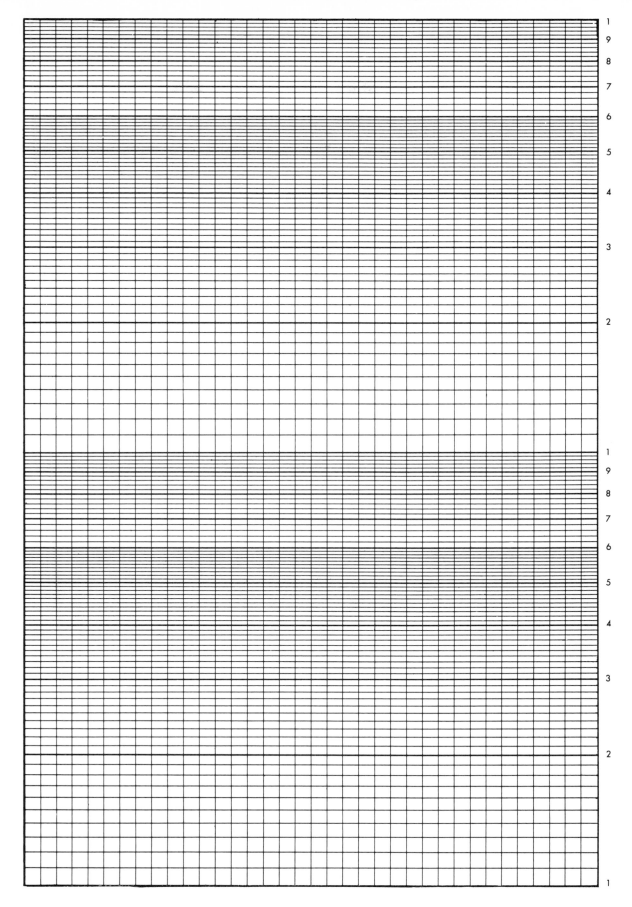

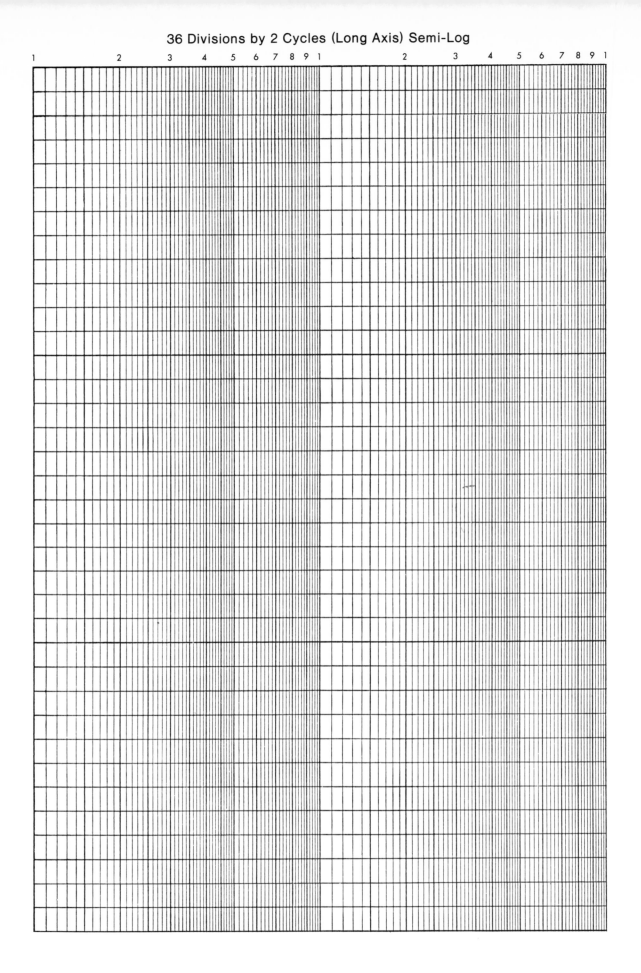

52 Divisions by 2 Cycle Semi-Log
(Months and quarters)

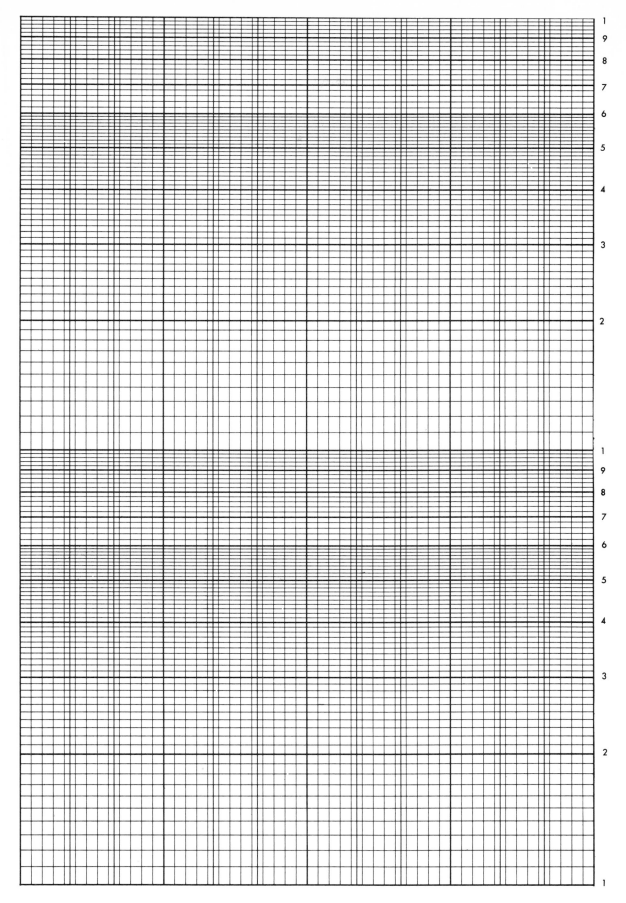

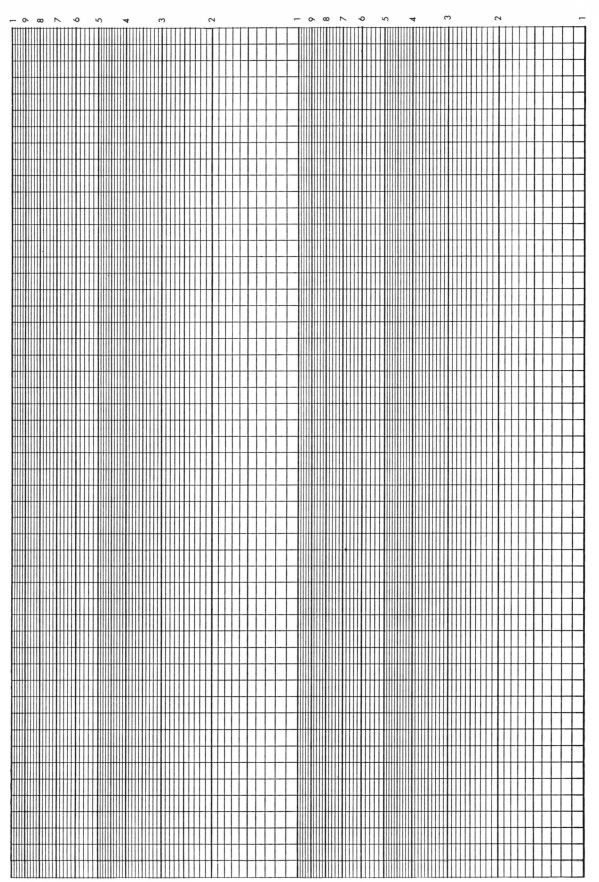

52 Divisions by 3 Cycle Semi-Log

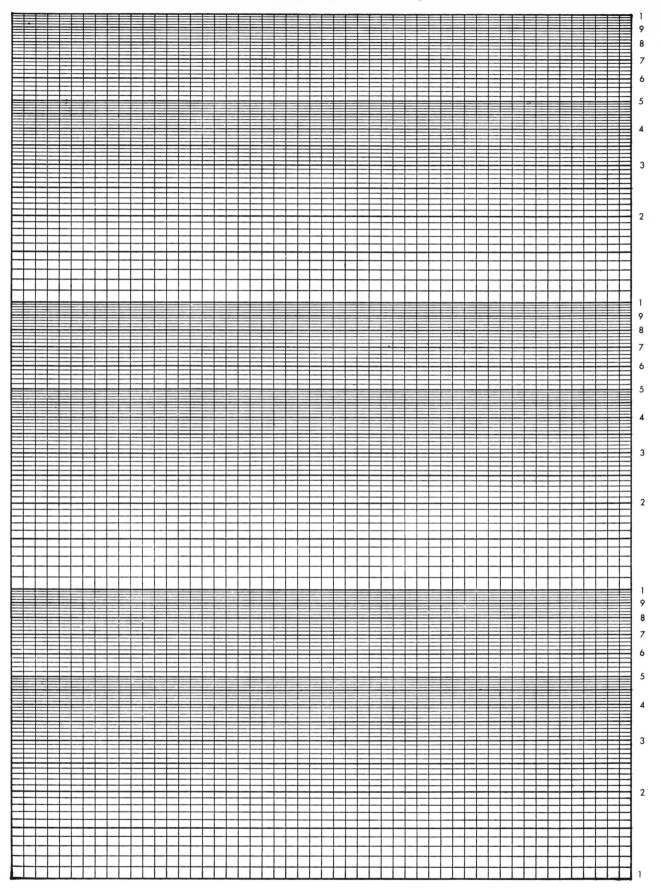

60 Divisions 6th Accent by 1 Cycle Semi-Log

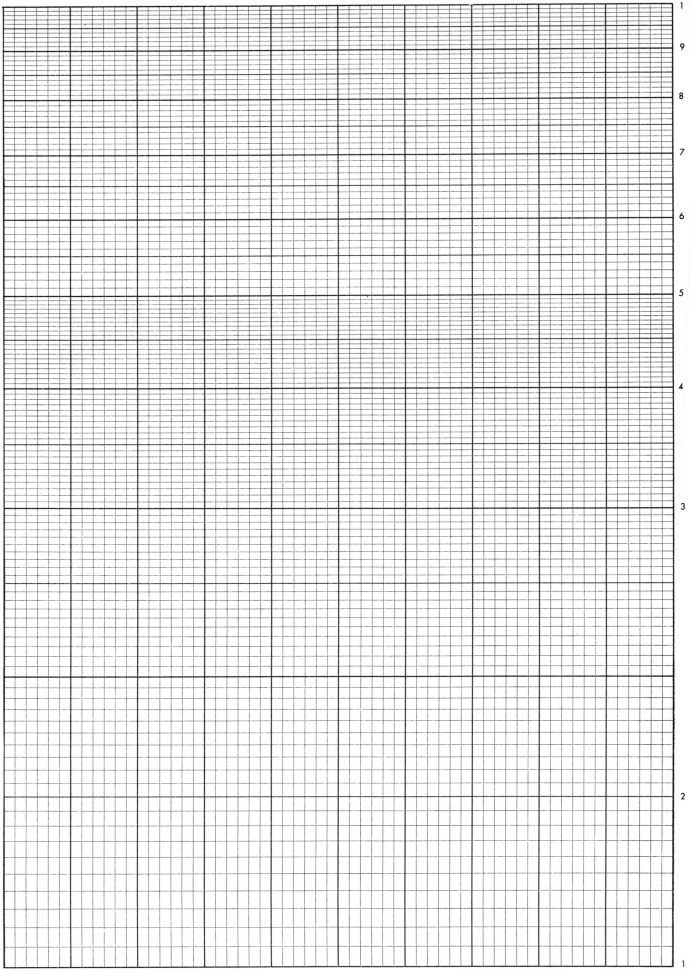

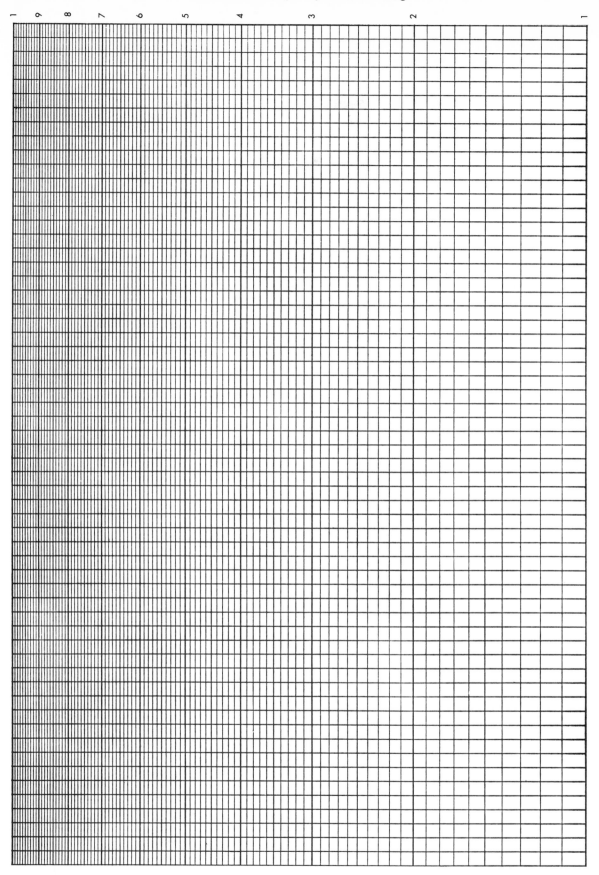

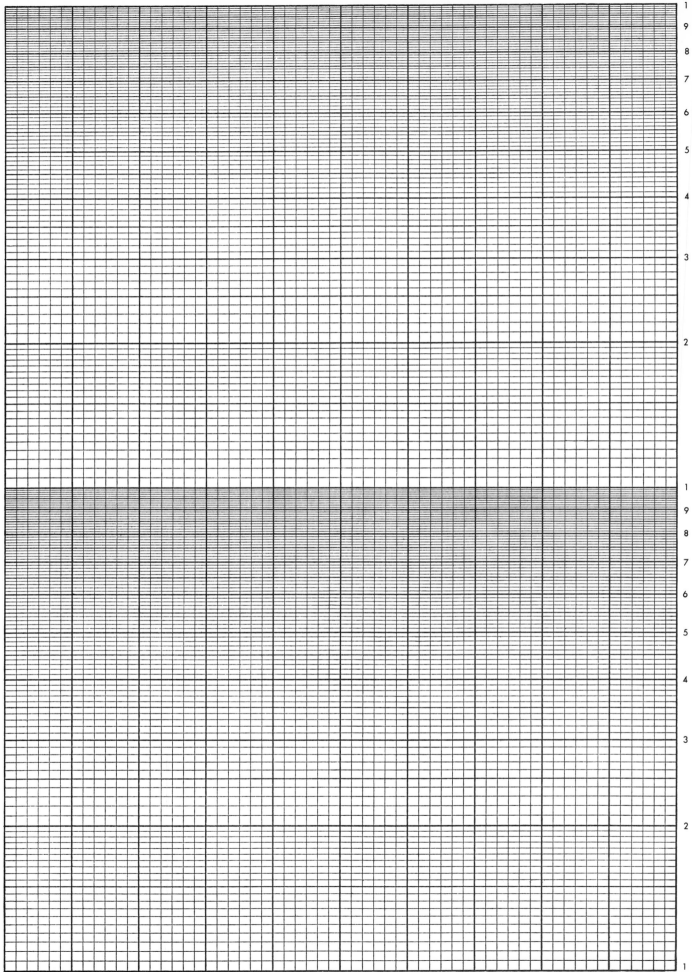

GRAPH PAPER From Your COPIER—**HPBooks**

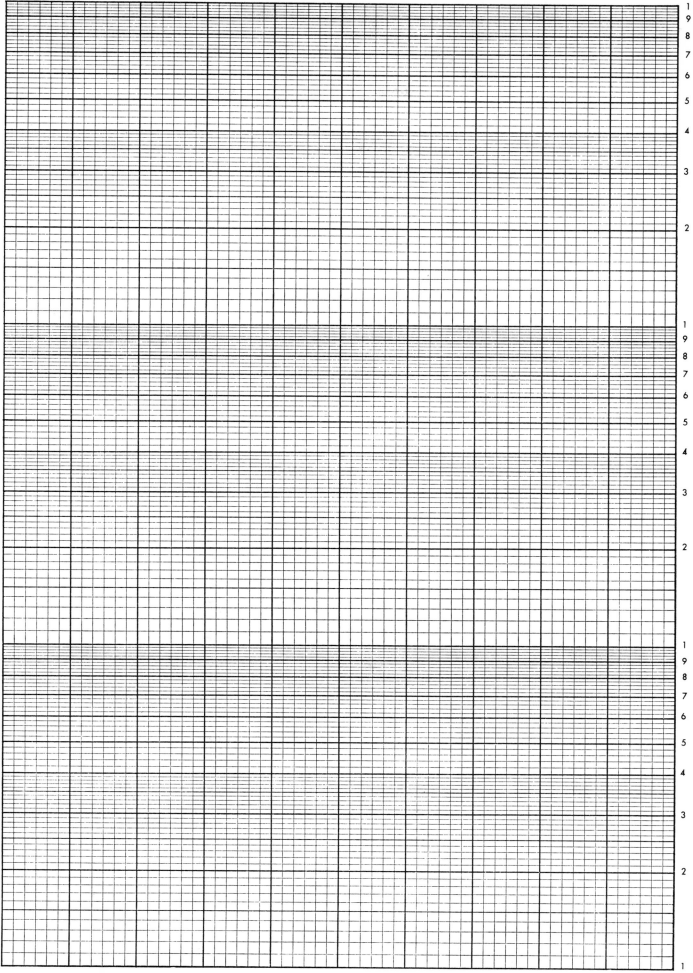

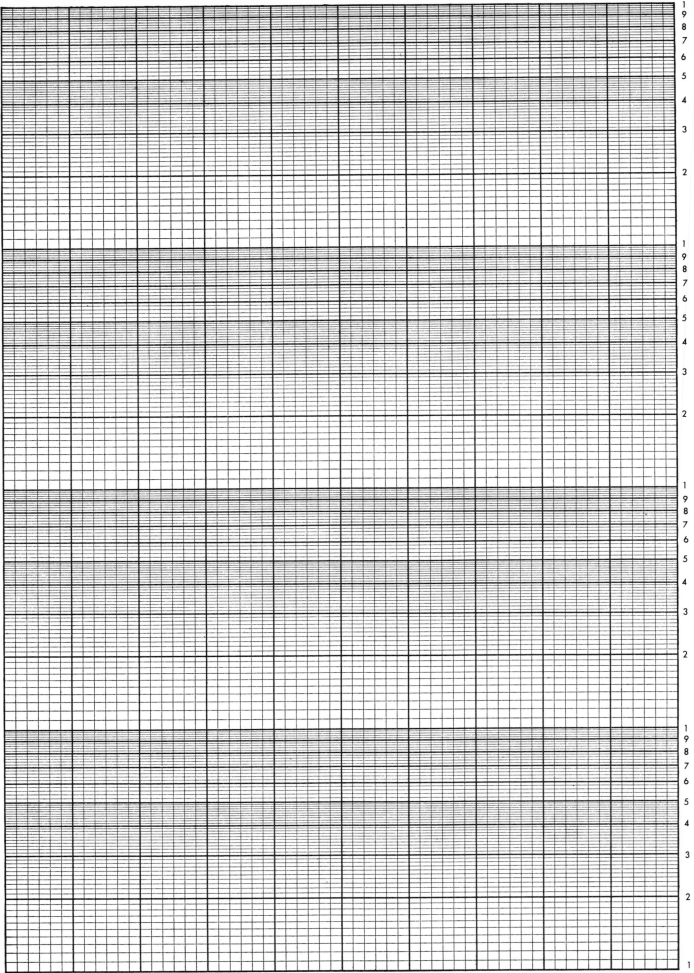

70 Divisions 5th, 10th Accent by 1 Cycle Semi-Log

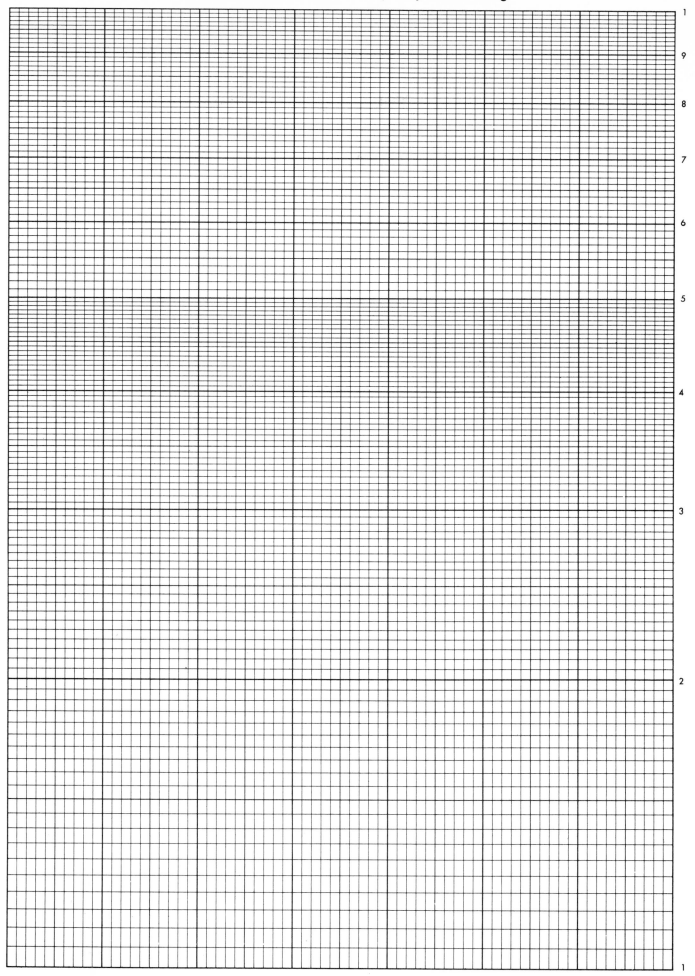

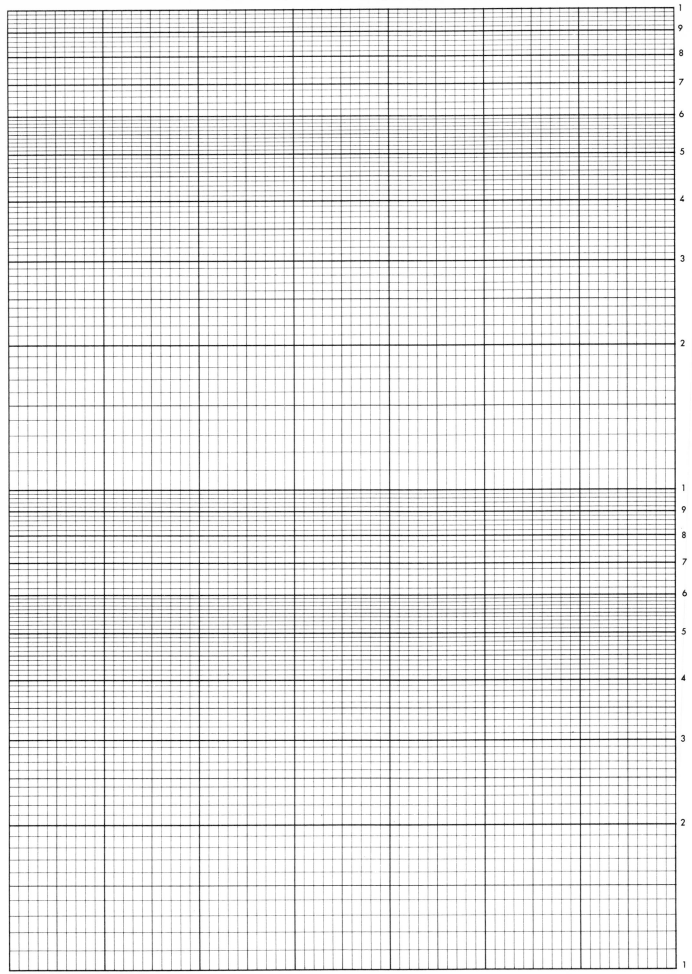

GRAPH PAPER From Your COPIER—**HPBooks**

70 Divisions 5th, 10th Accent by 3 Cycle Semi-Log

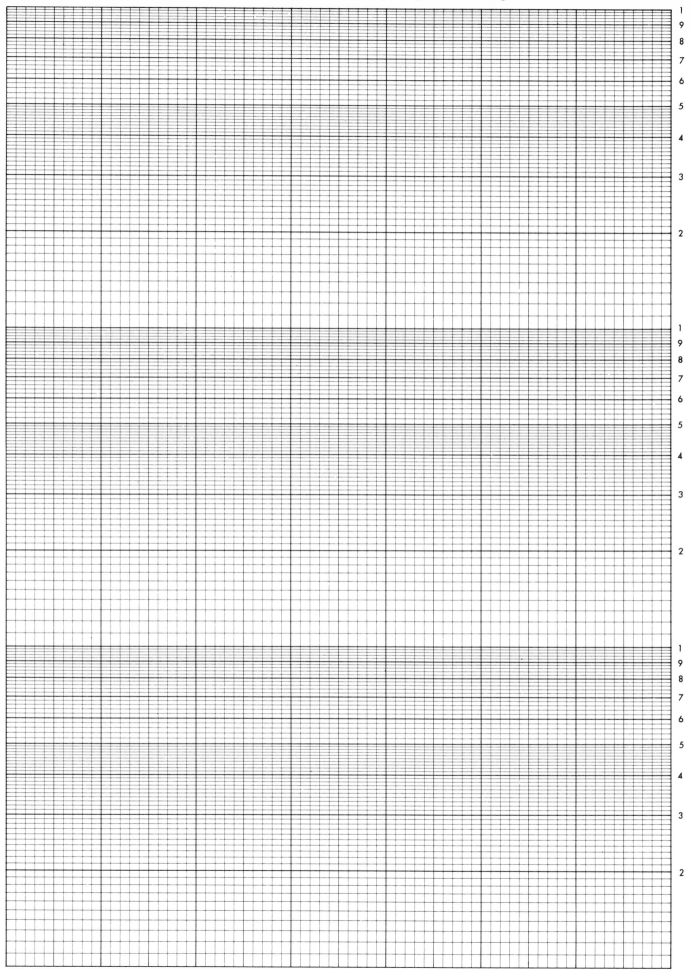

70 Divisions 5th, 10th Accent by 4 Cycle Semi-Log

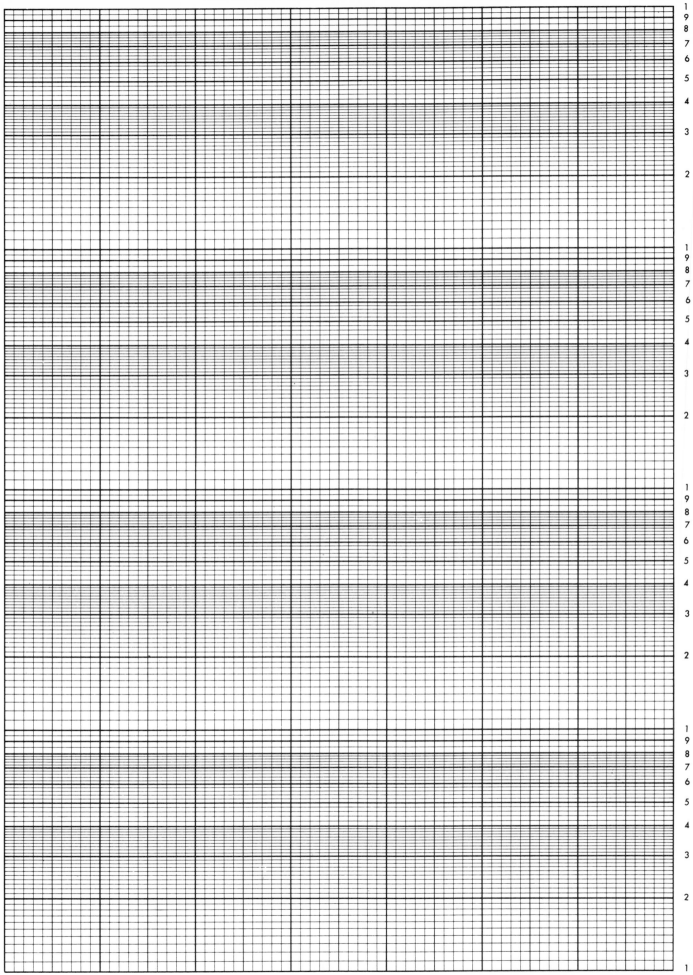

GRAPH PAPER From Your COPIER—**HPBooks**

70 Divisions 5th, 10th Accent by 5 Cycle Semi-Log

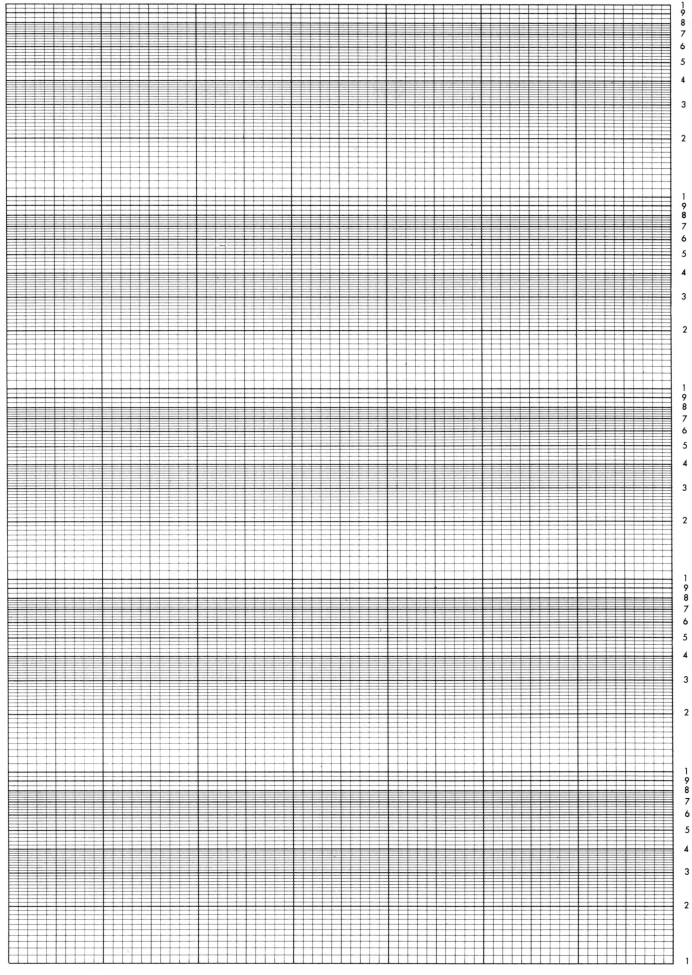

70 Divisions 5th, 10th Accent by 6 Cycle Semi-Log

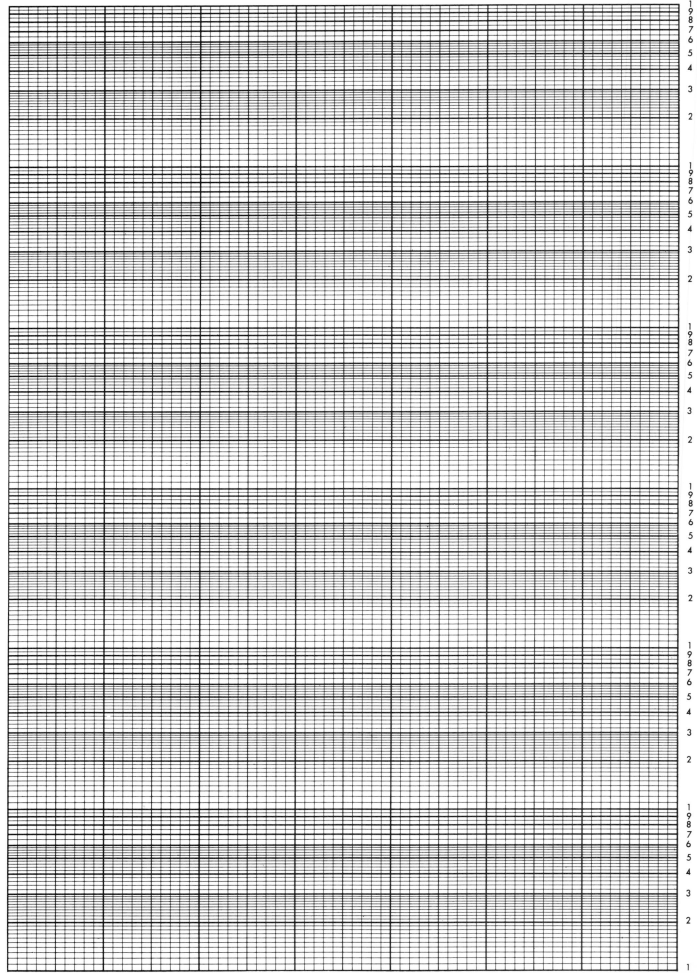

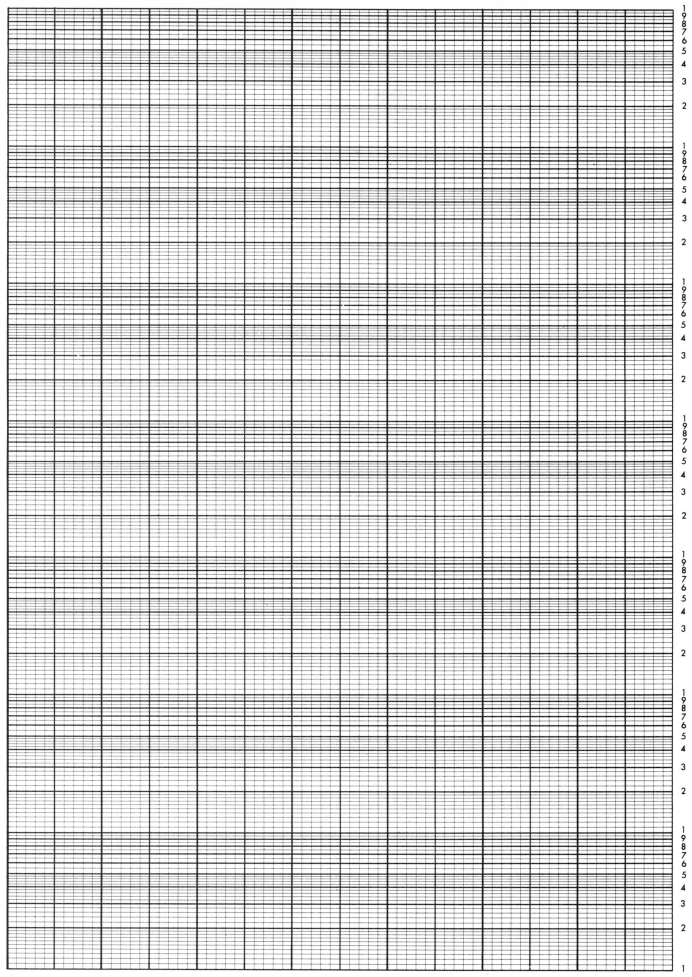

70 Divisions 5th, 10th Accent by 8 Cycle Semi-Log

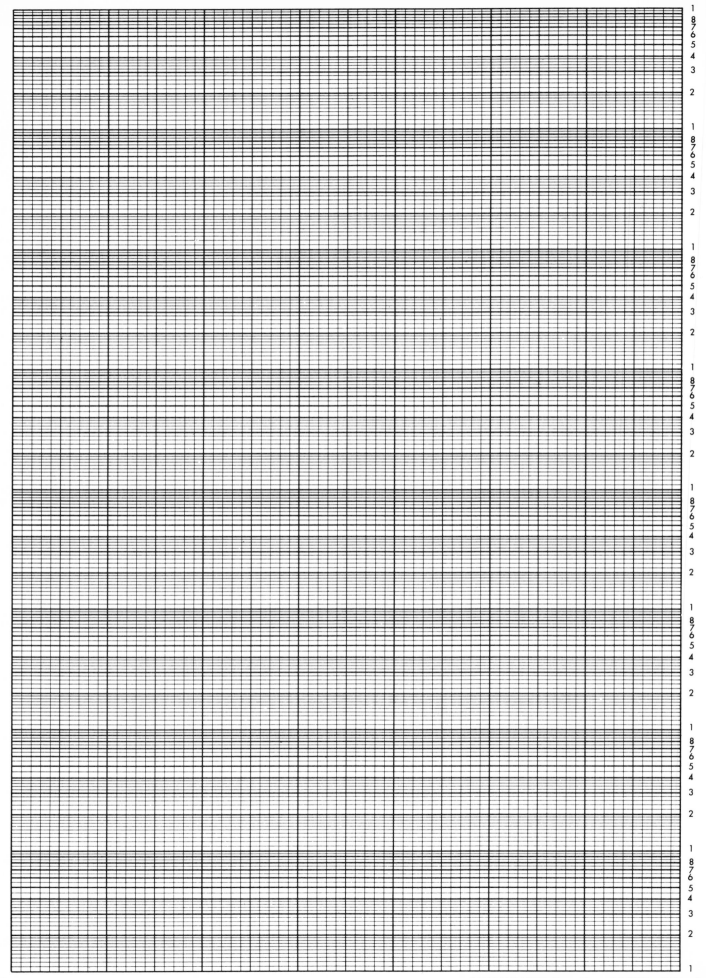

70 Divisions 5th, 10th Accent by 10 Cycle Semi-Log

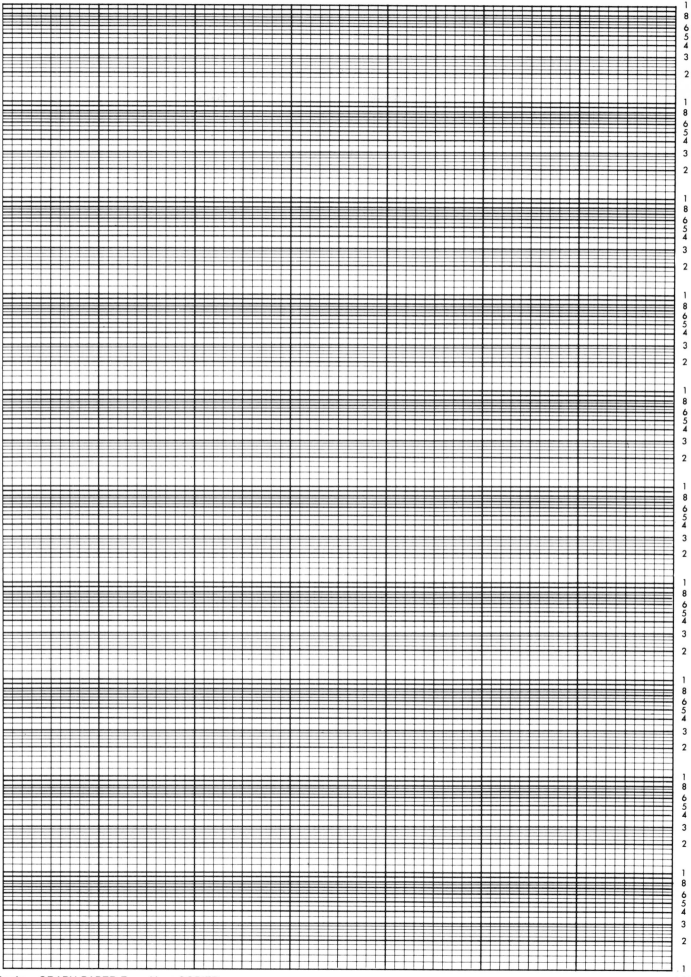

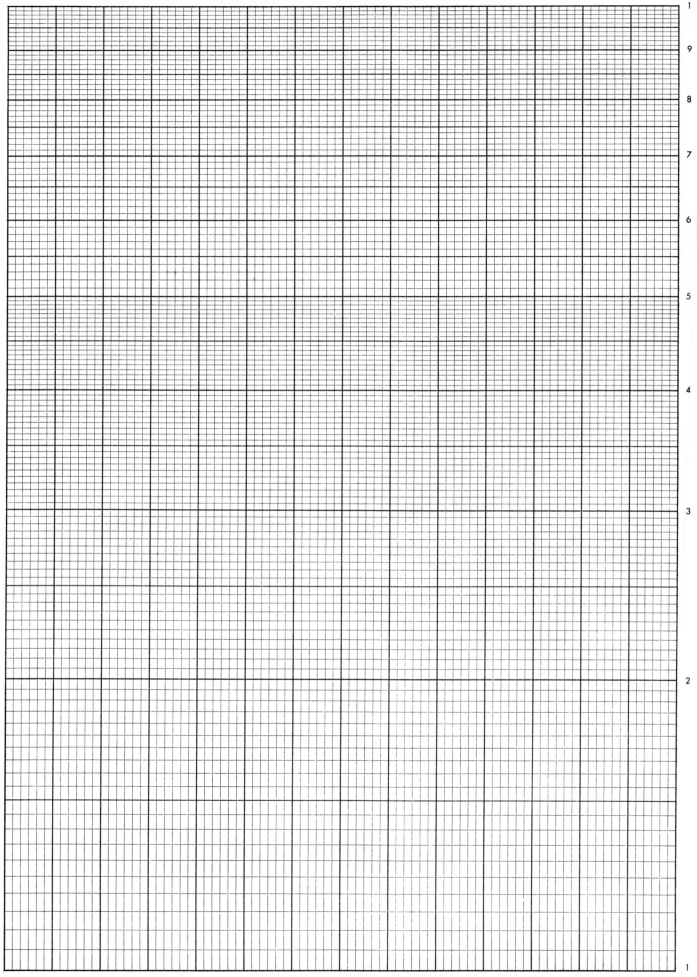

GRAPH PAPER From Your COPIER—**HPBooks**

84 Divisions 6th Accent by 2 Cycle Semi-Log

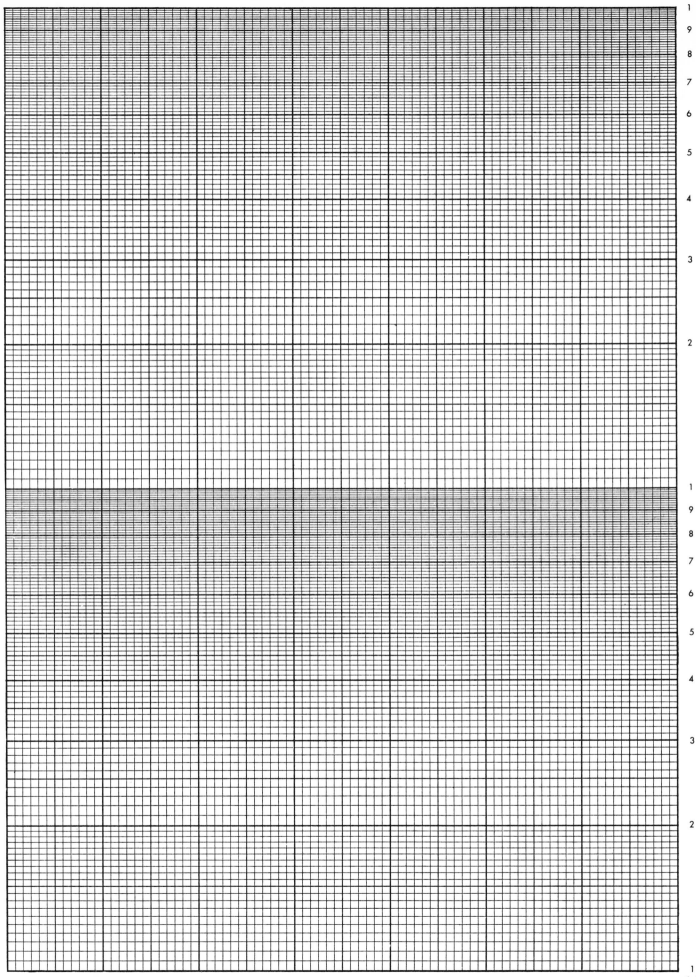

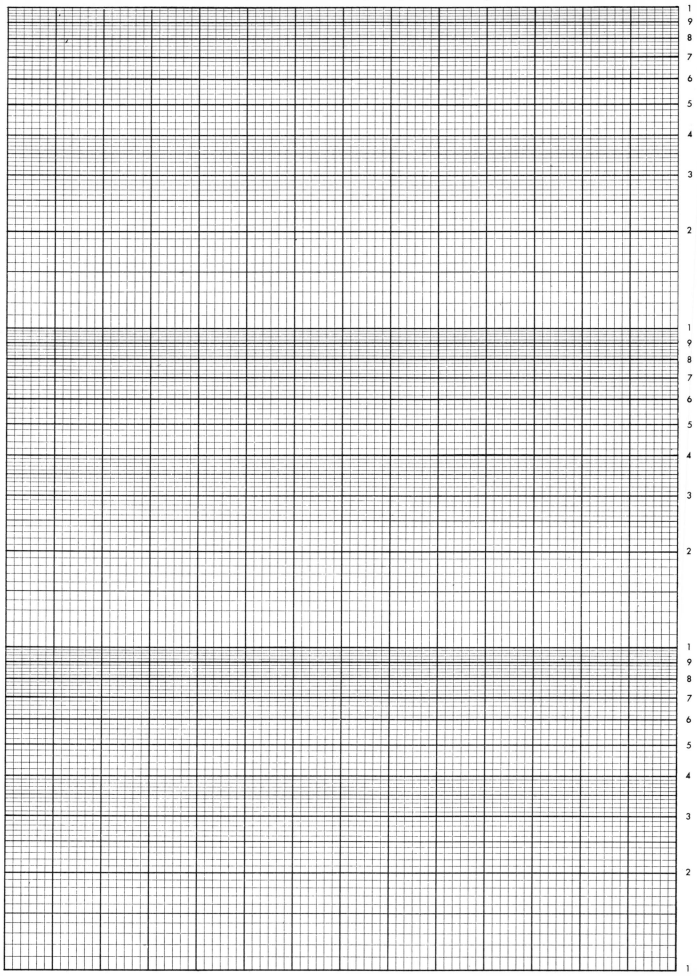

84 Divisions 6th, 12th Accent by 4 Cycle Semi-Log

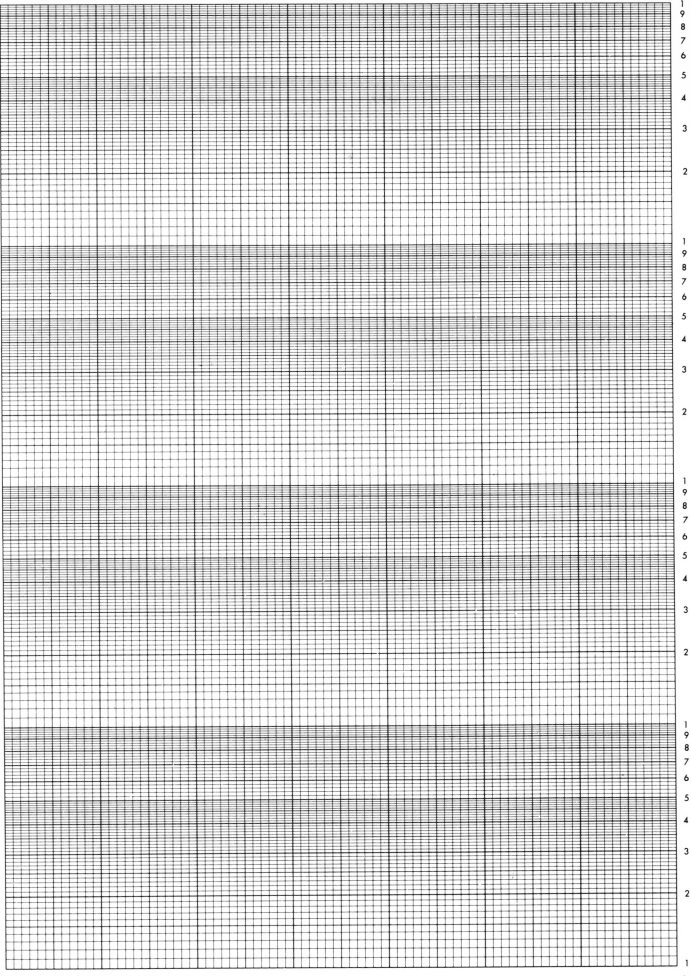

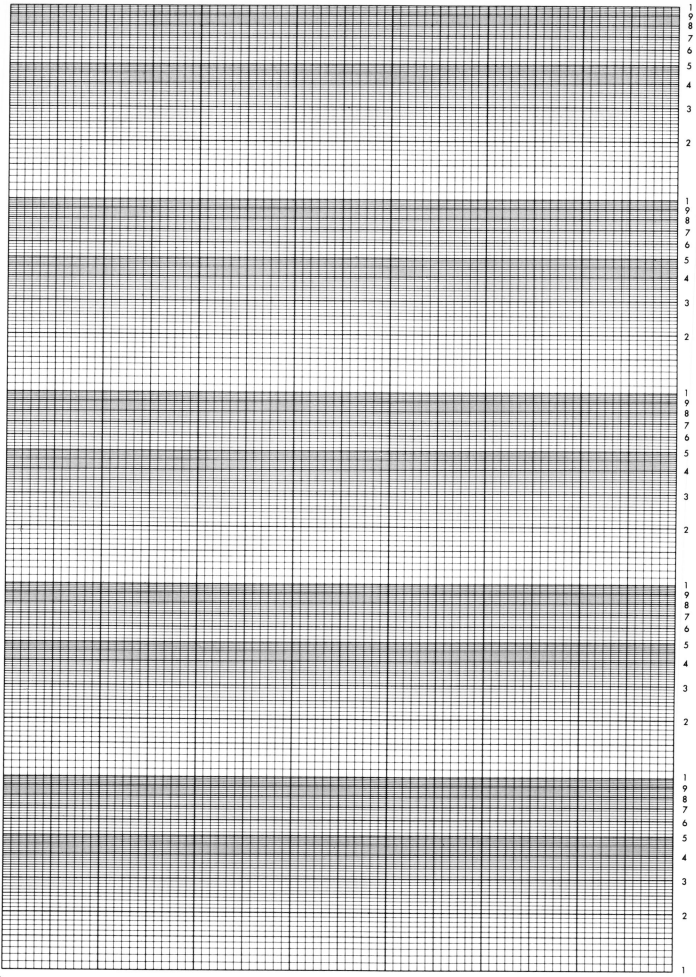

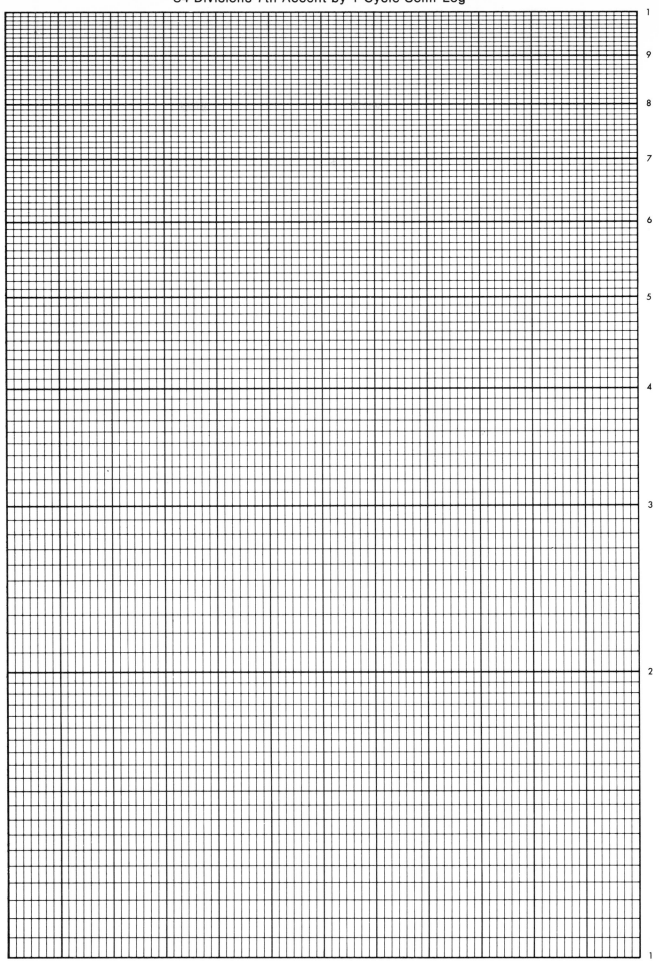

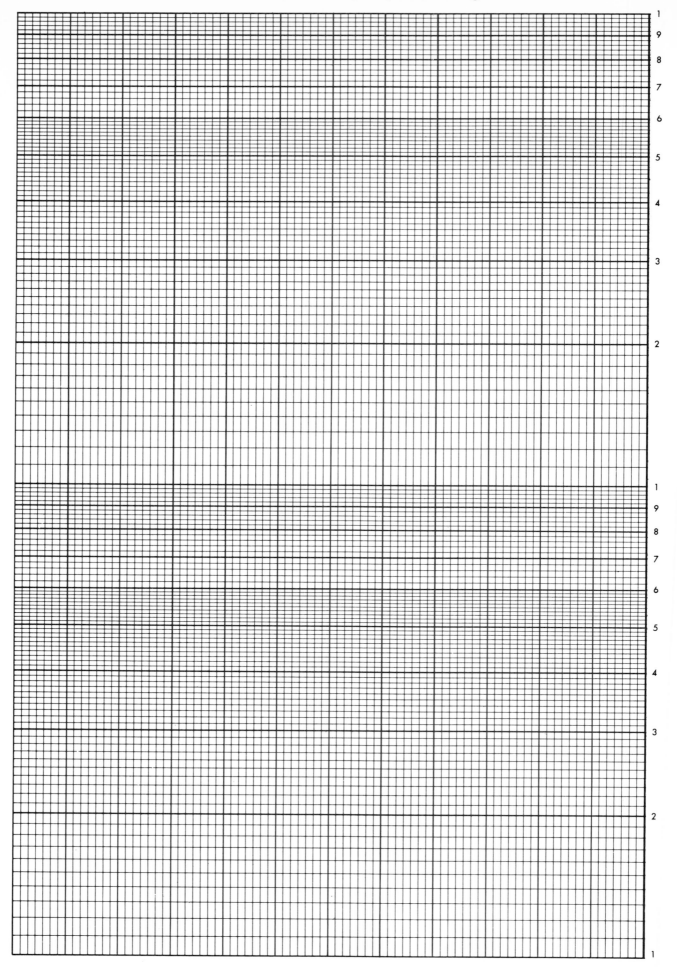

84 Divisions 7th Accent by 2 Cycle Semi-Log

84 Divisions 7th Accent by 3 Cycle Semi-Log

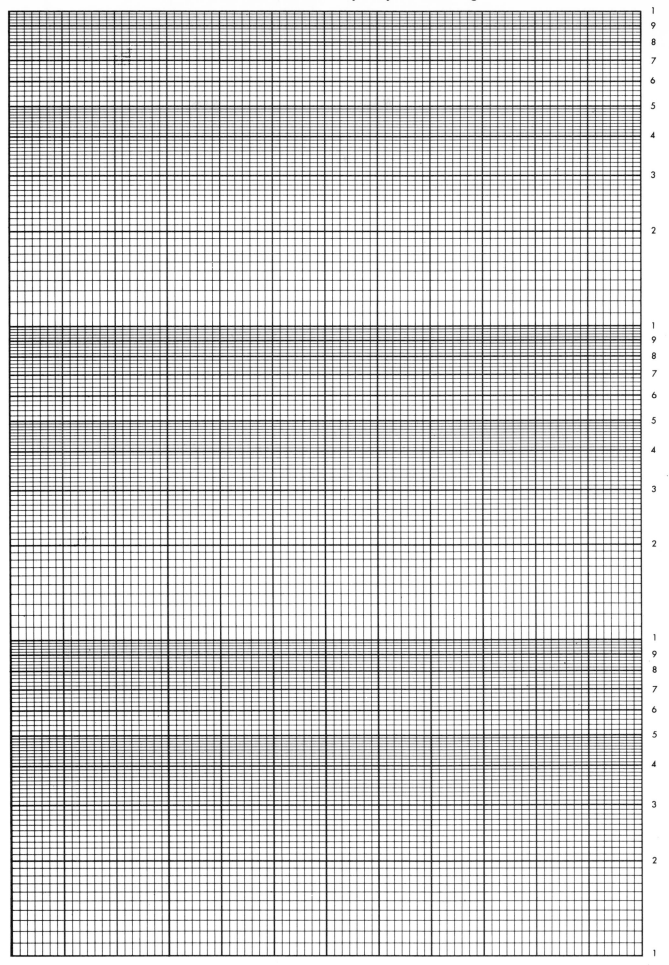

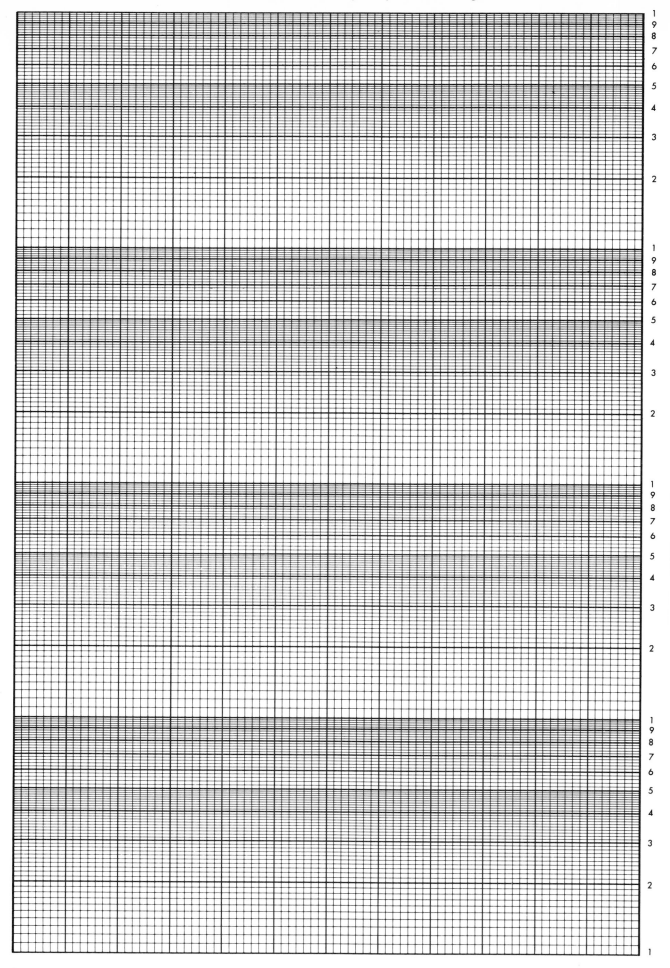

GRAPH PAPER From Your COPIER—**HPBooks**

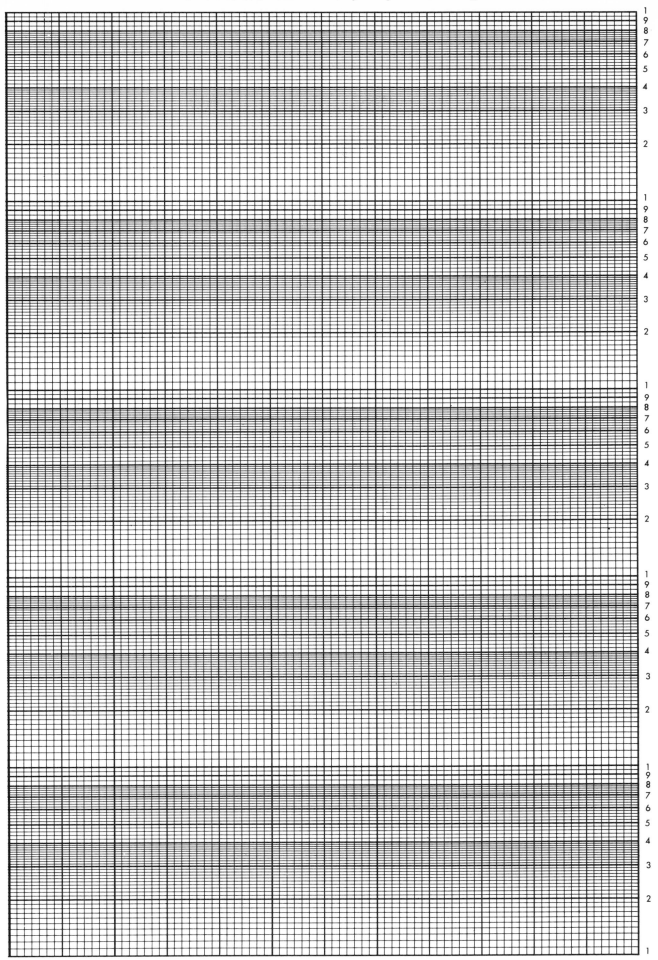

84 Divisions 7th Accent by 6 Cycle Semi-Log

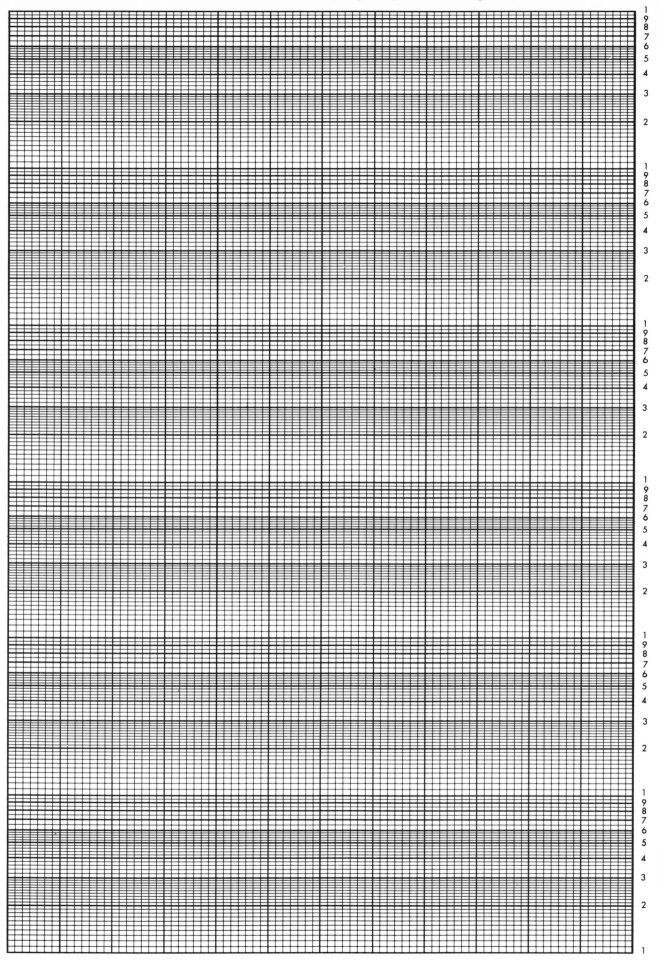

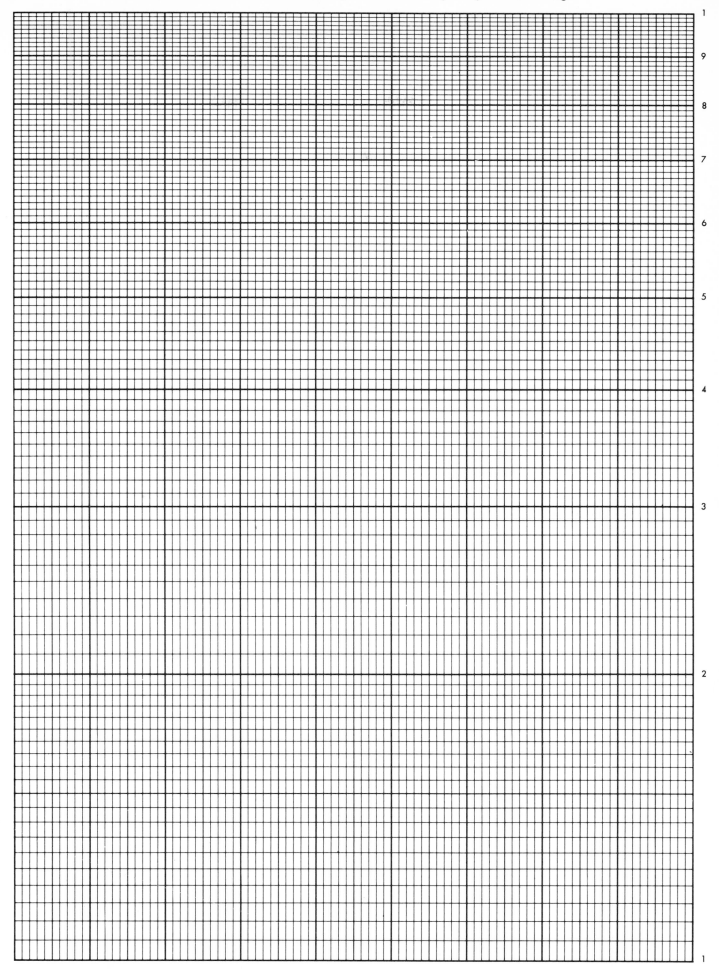

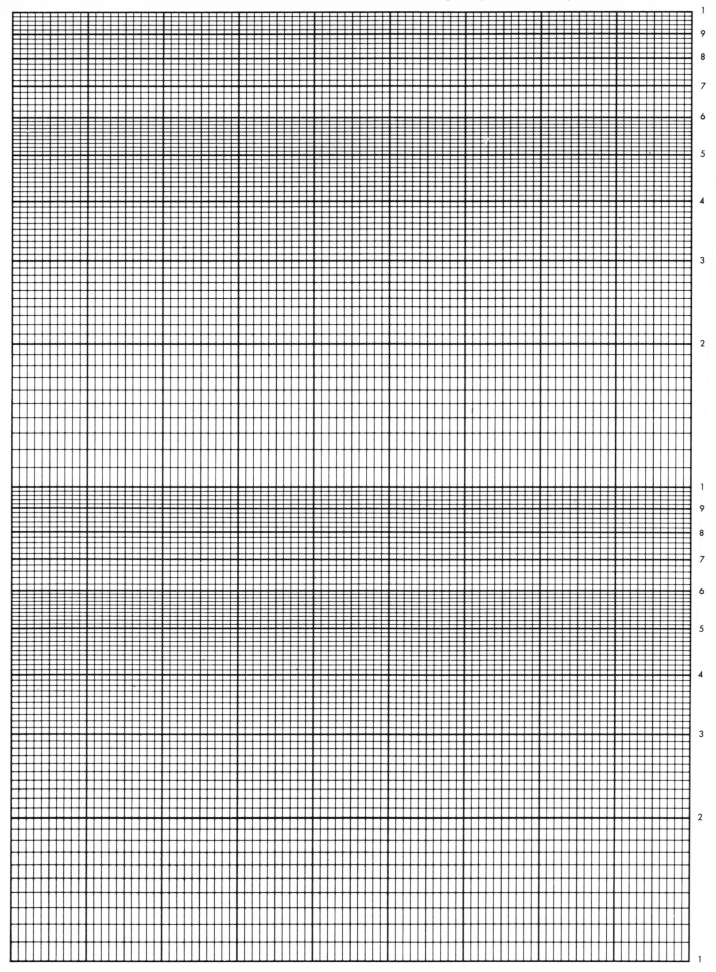

GRAPH PAPER From Your COPIER—**HPBooks**

90 Divisions (2 millimeters) 5th, 10th Accent by 3 Cycle Semi-Log

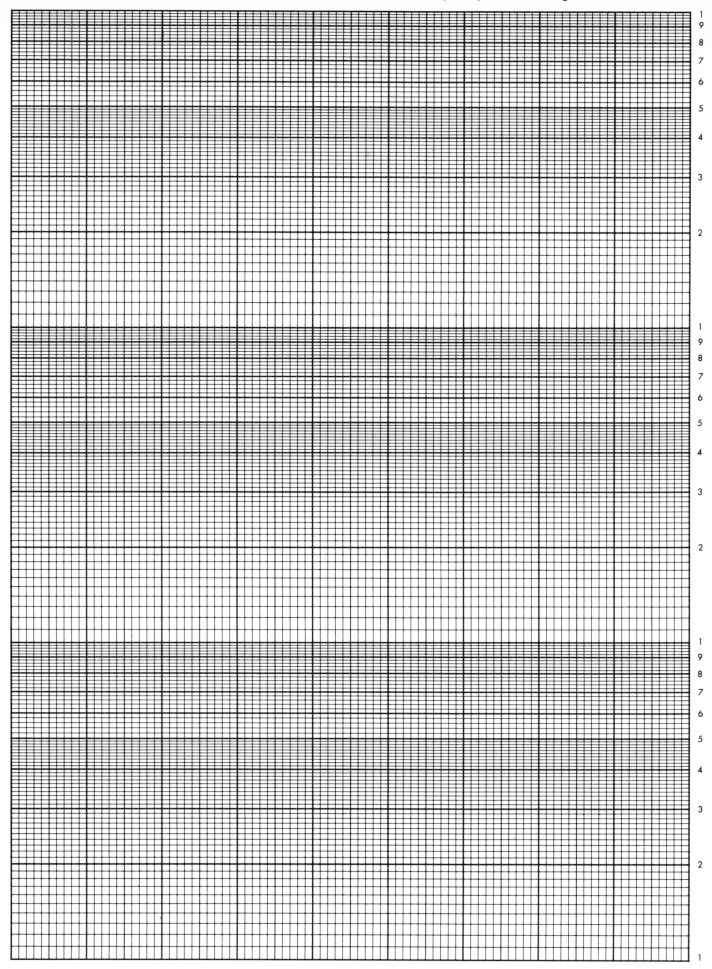

90 Divisions (2 millimeters) 5th, 10th Accent by 4 Cycle Semi-Log

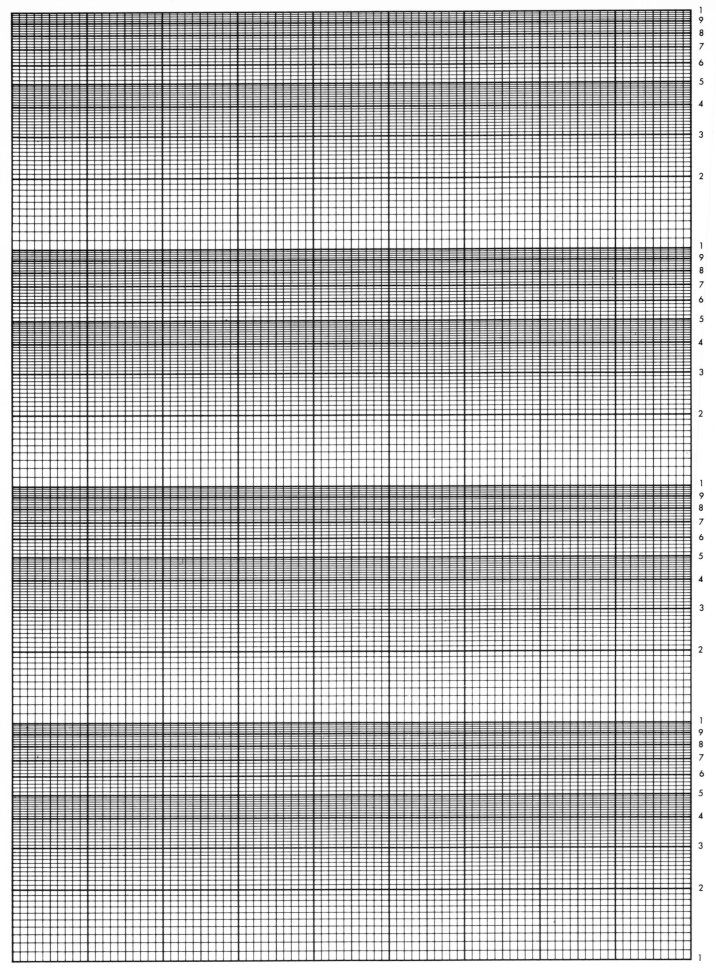

GRAPH PAPER From Your COPIER—**HPBooks**

90 Divisions (2 millimeters) 5th, 10th Accent by 5 Cycle Semi-Log

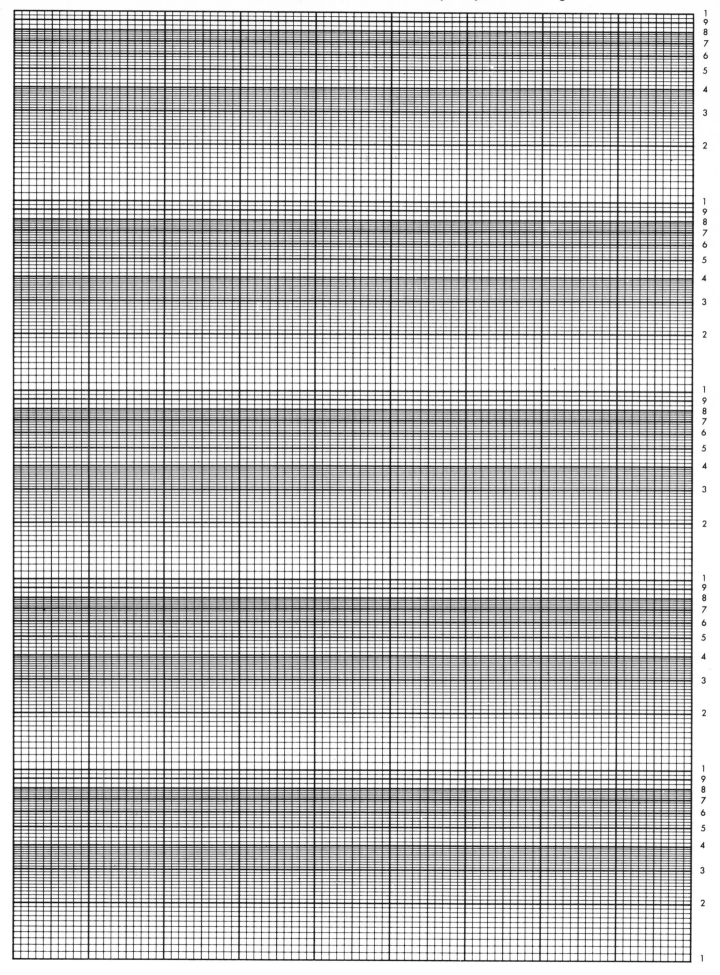

90 Divisions (2 millimeters) 5th, 10th Accent by 6 Cycle Semi-Log

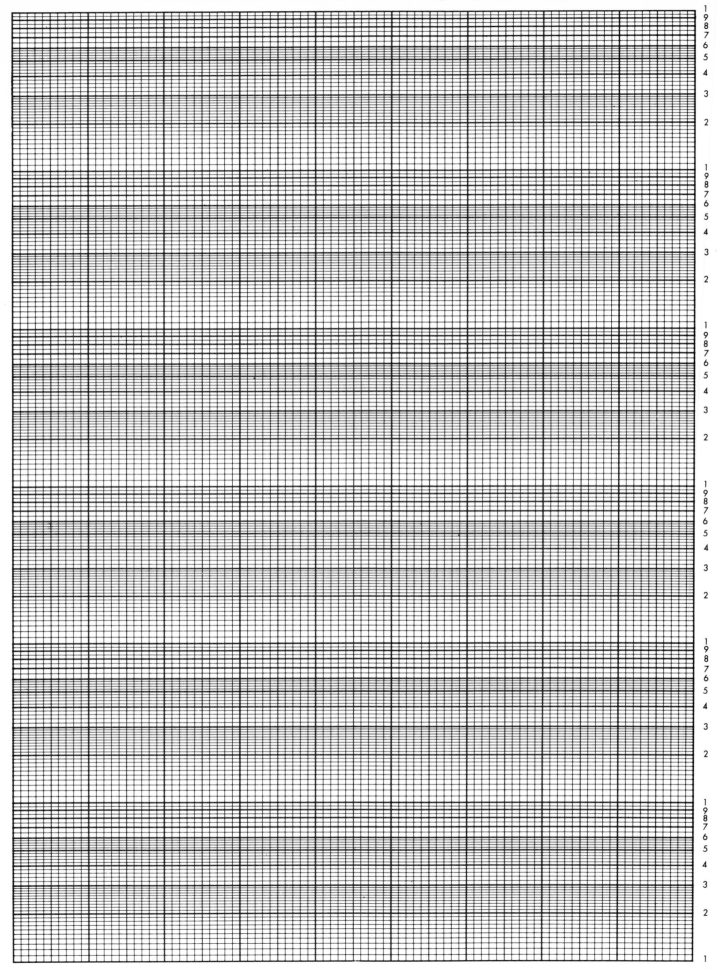

GRAPH PAPER From Your COPIER—**HPBooks**

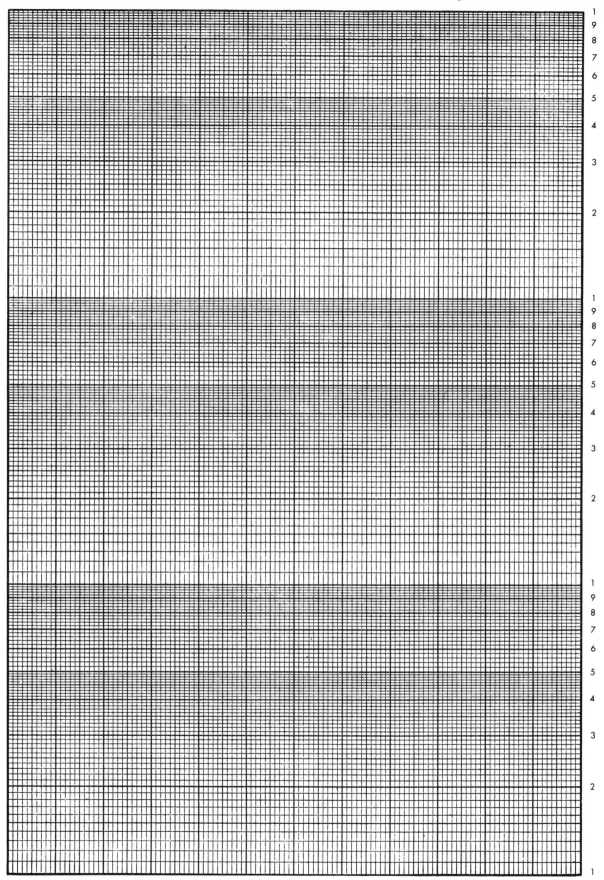

120 Divisions 5th, 10th Accent by 4 Cycle Semi-Log

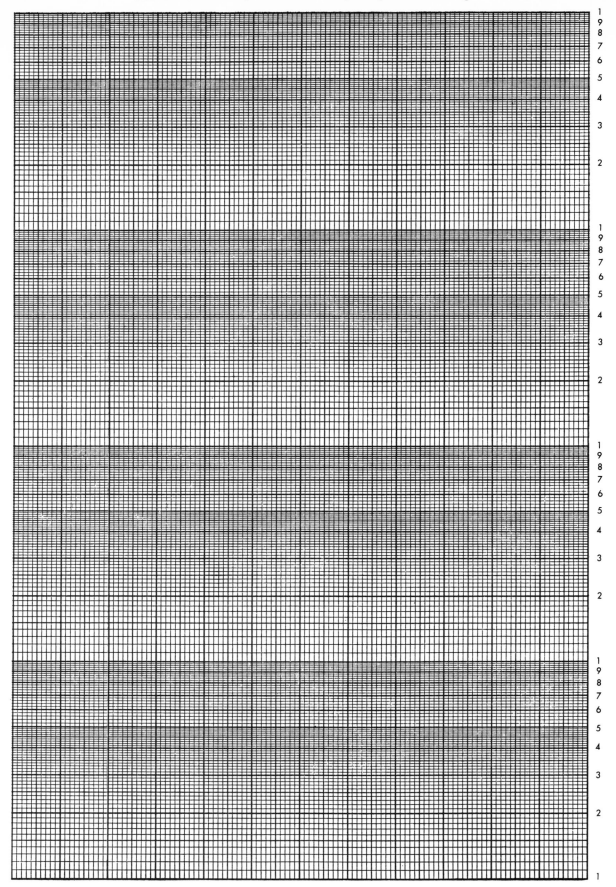

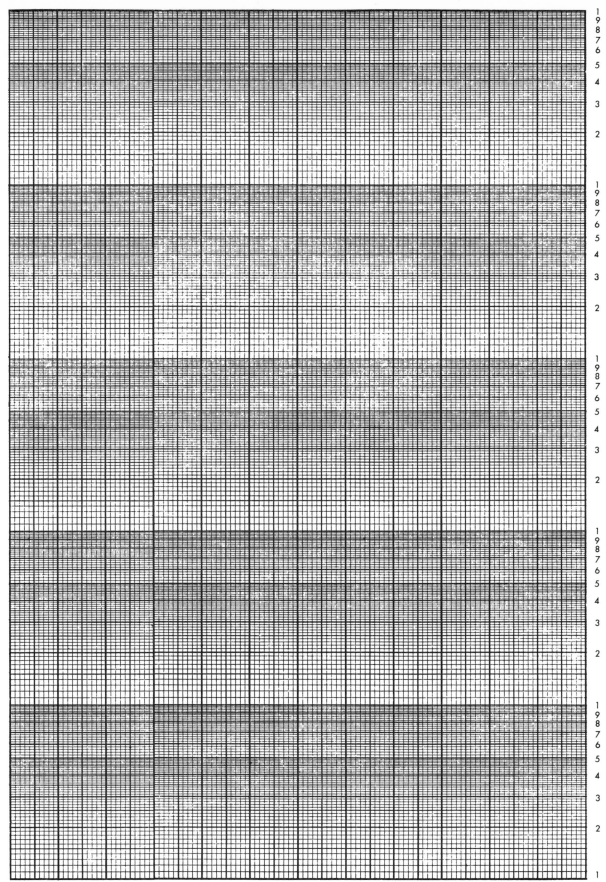

120 Divisions 5th, 10th Accent by 6 Cycle Semi-Log

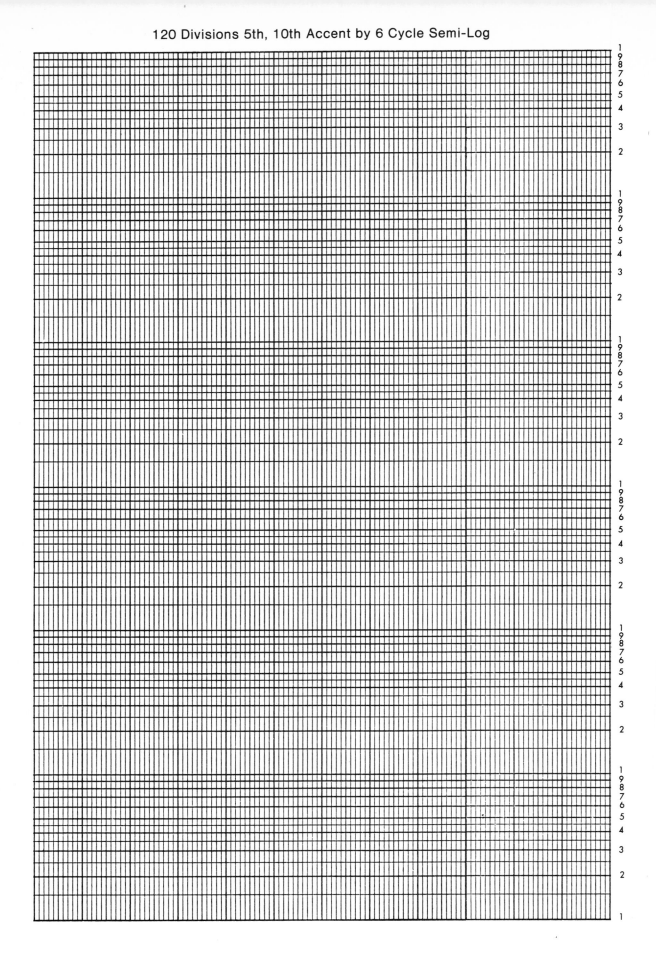

GRAPH PAPER From Your COPIER—**HPBooks**

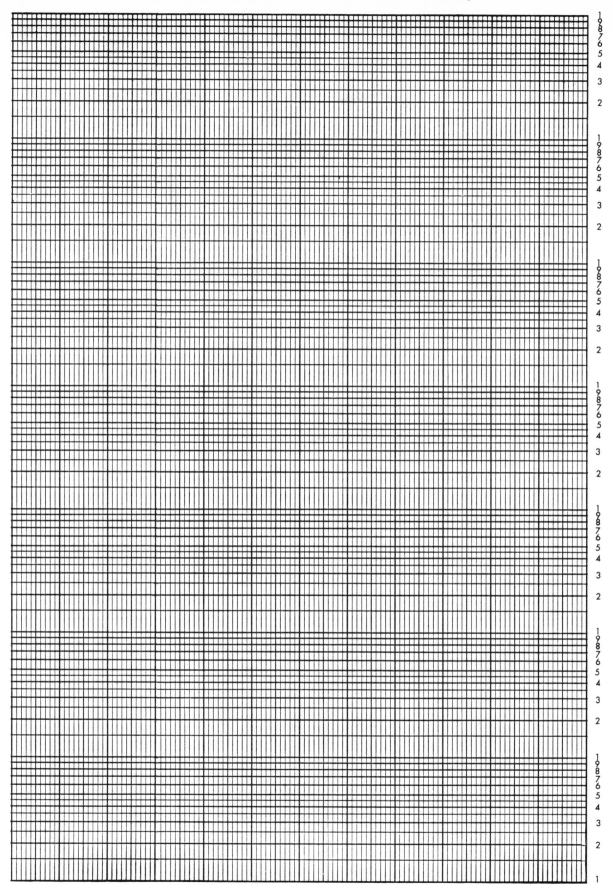

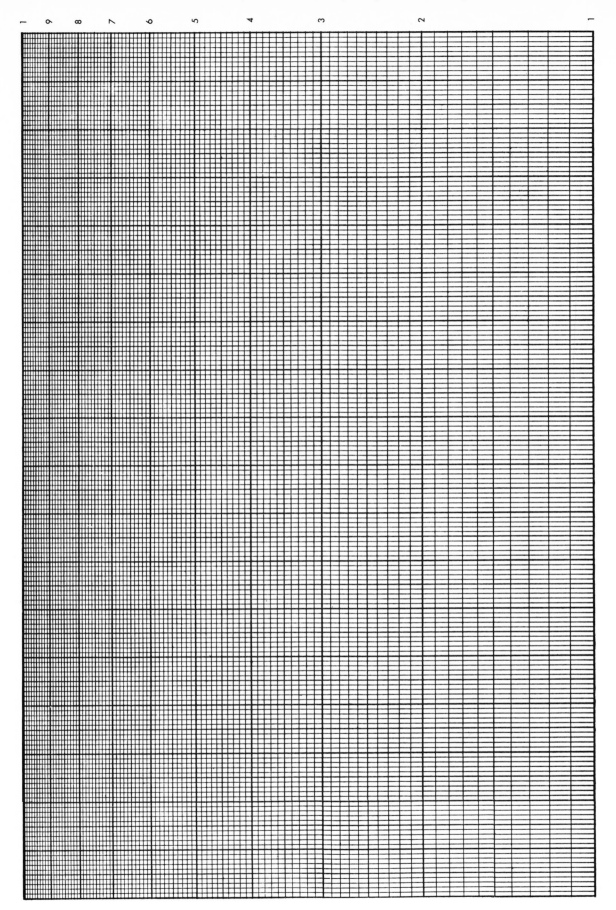

180 Divisions (1 millimeter) 5th, 10th Accent by 1 Cycle Semi-Log

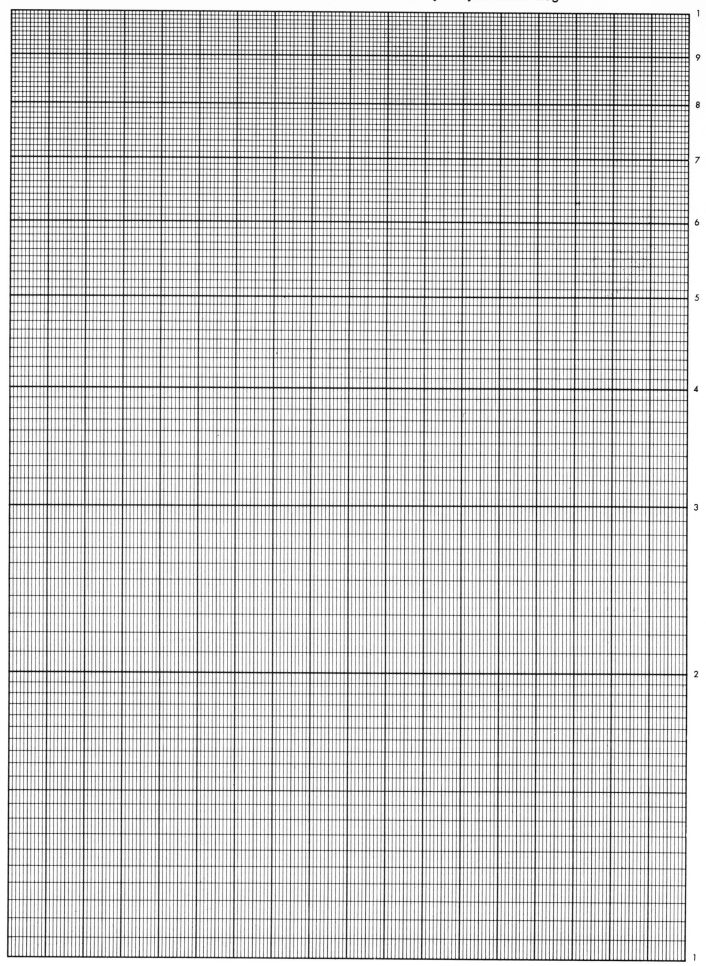

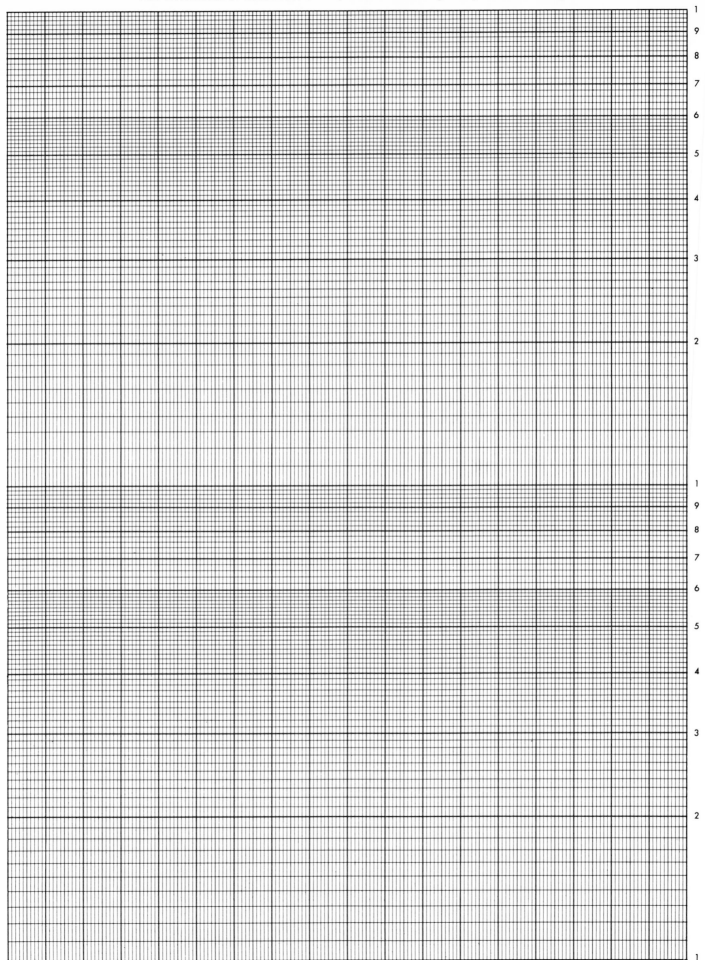

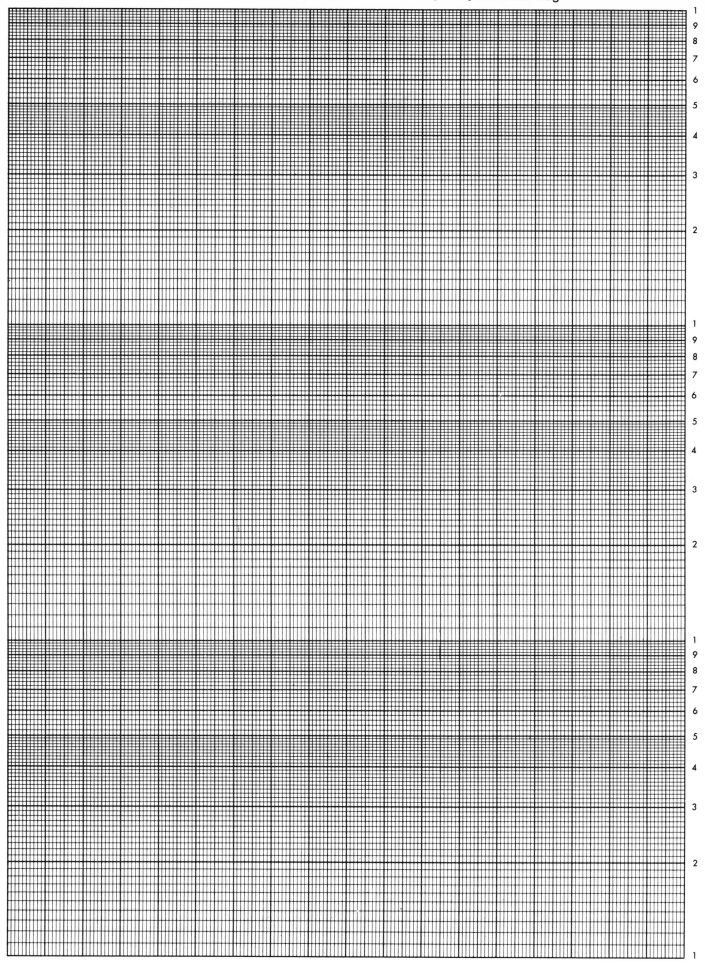

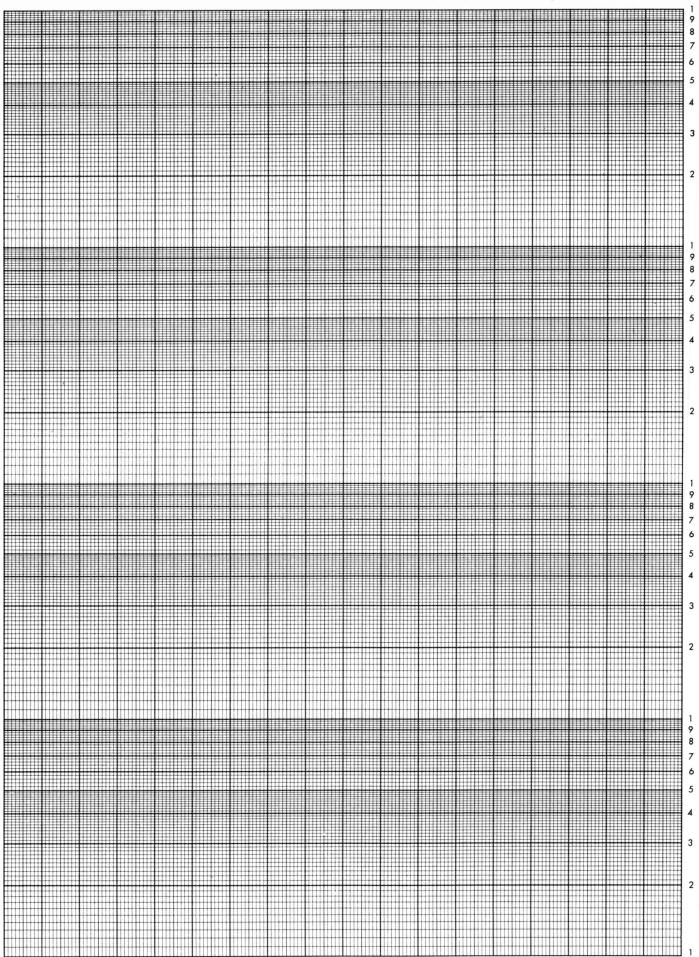

180 Divisions (1 millimeter) 5th, 10th Accent by 5 Cycle Semi-Log

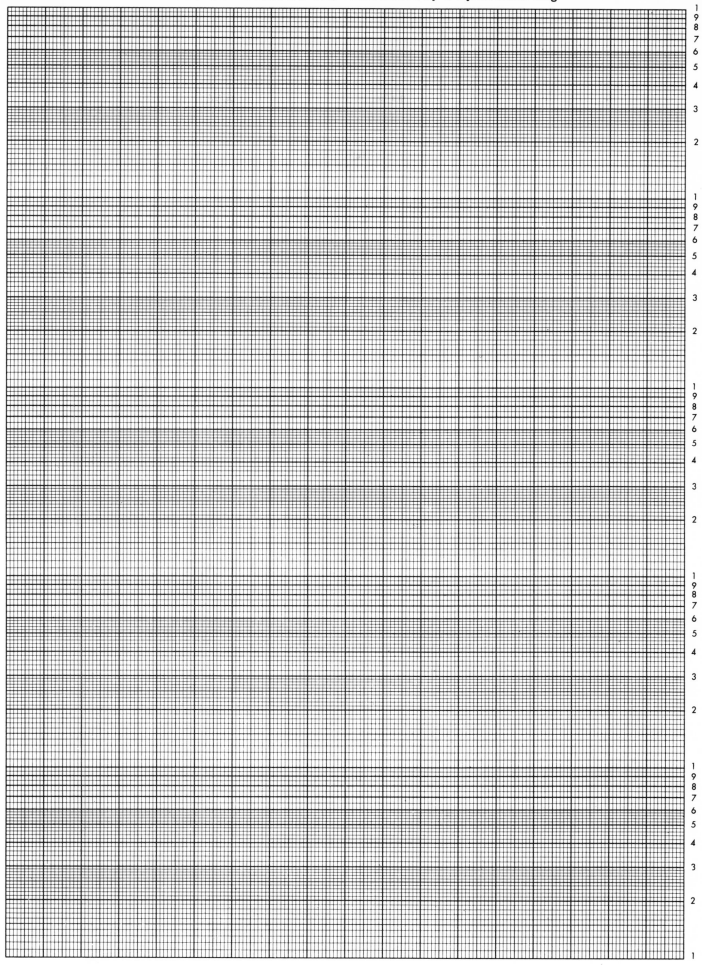

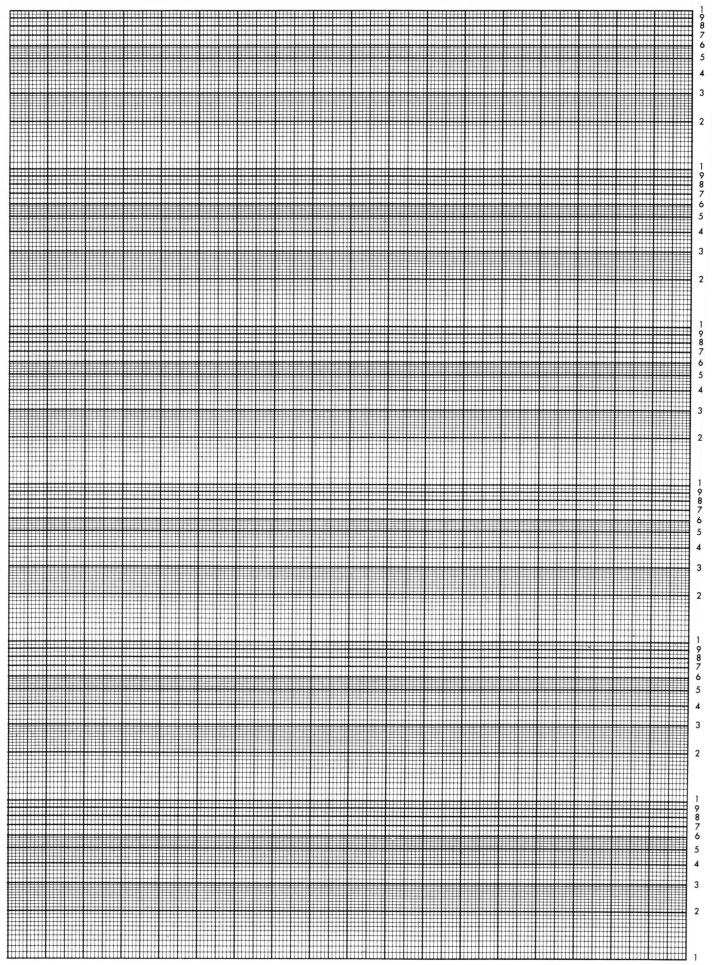

GRAPH PAPER From Your COPIER—**HPBooks**

180 Divisions (1 millimeter) 5th, 10th Accent by 7 Cycle Semi-Log

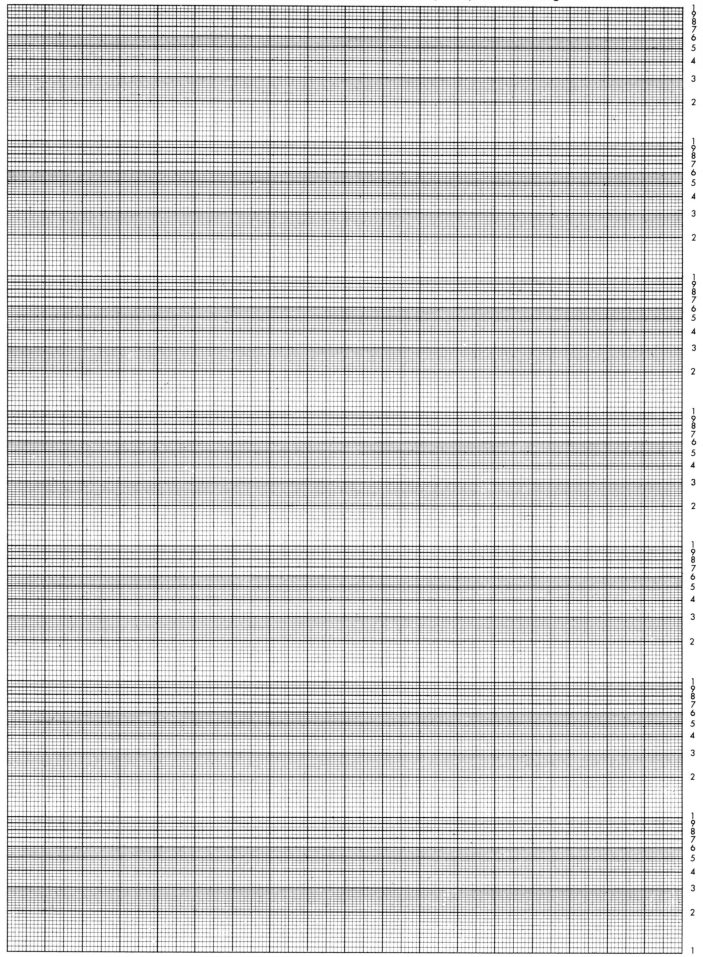

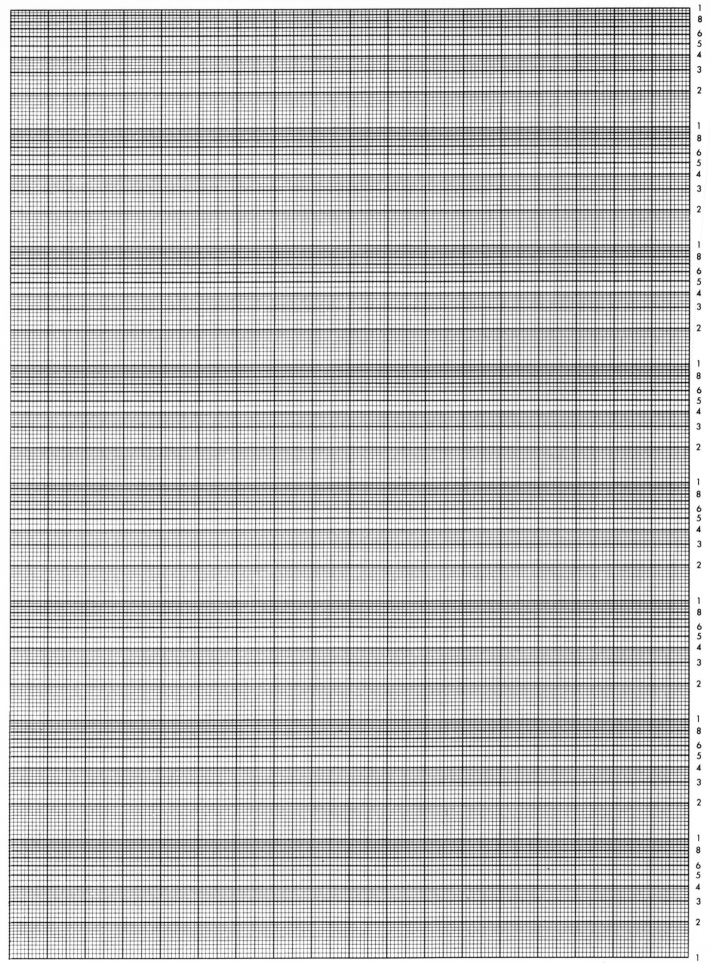

180 Divisions (1 millimeter) 5th, 10th Accent by 10 Cycle Semi-Log

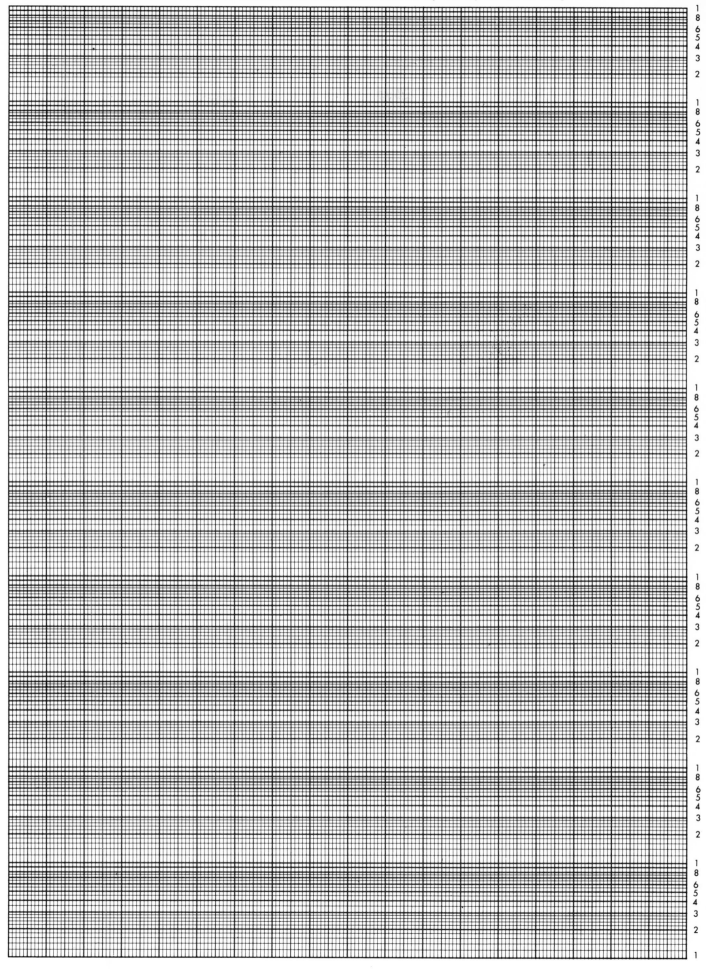

366 Divisions 5th Day & Month Accent by 1 Cycle Semi-Log

GRAPH PAPER From Your COPIER—**HPBooks**

1 Cycle by 1 Cycle Log-Log

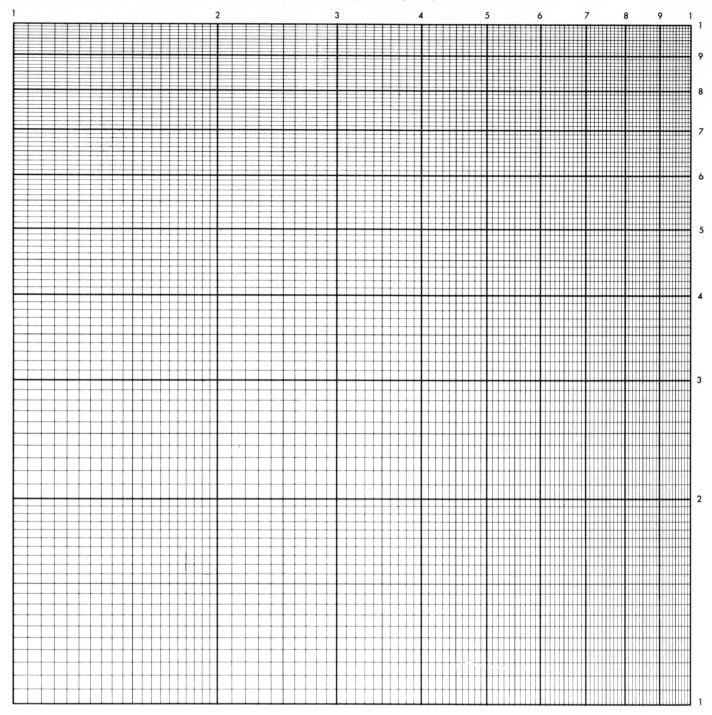

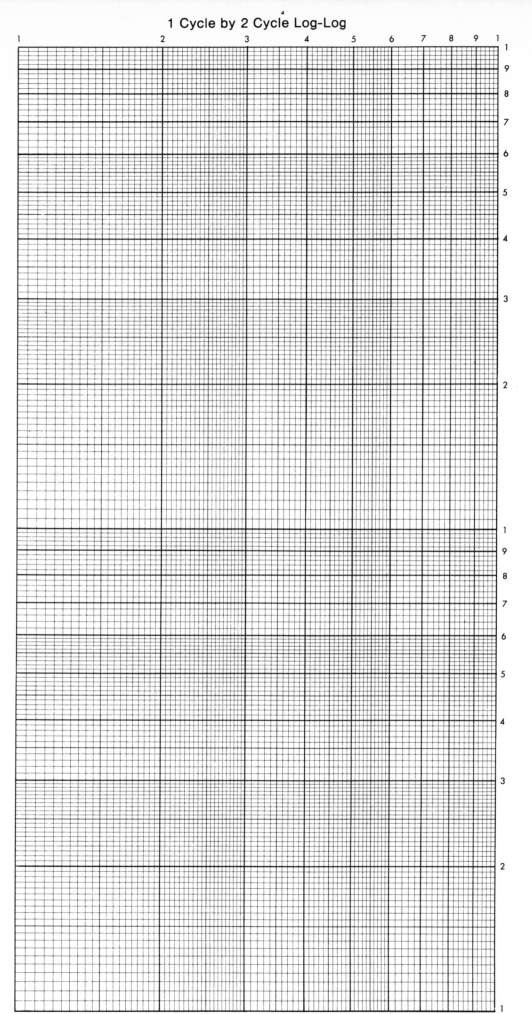

1 Cycle by 3 Cycle Log-Log

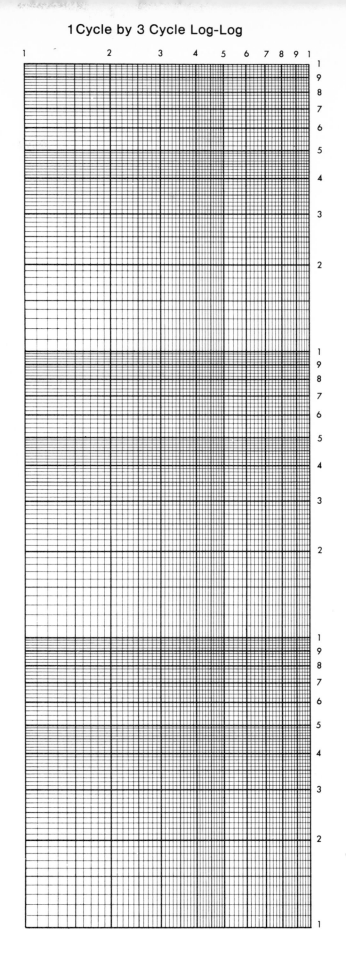

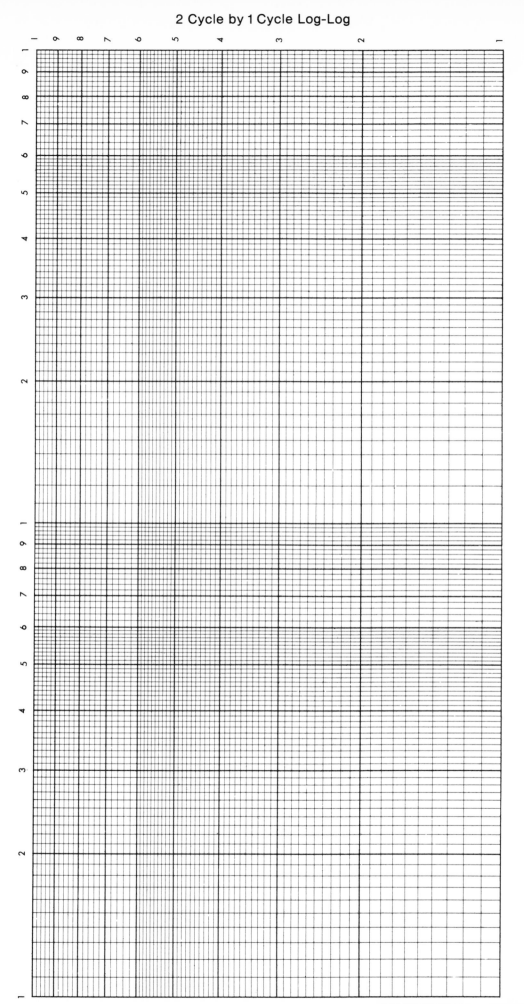

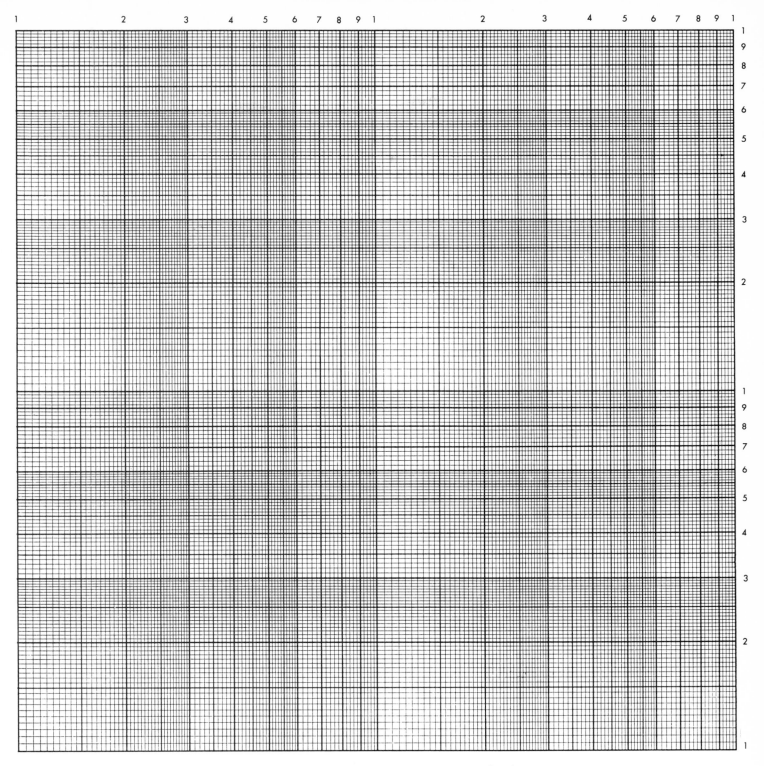

2 Cycle by 3 Cycle Log-Log

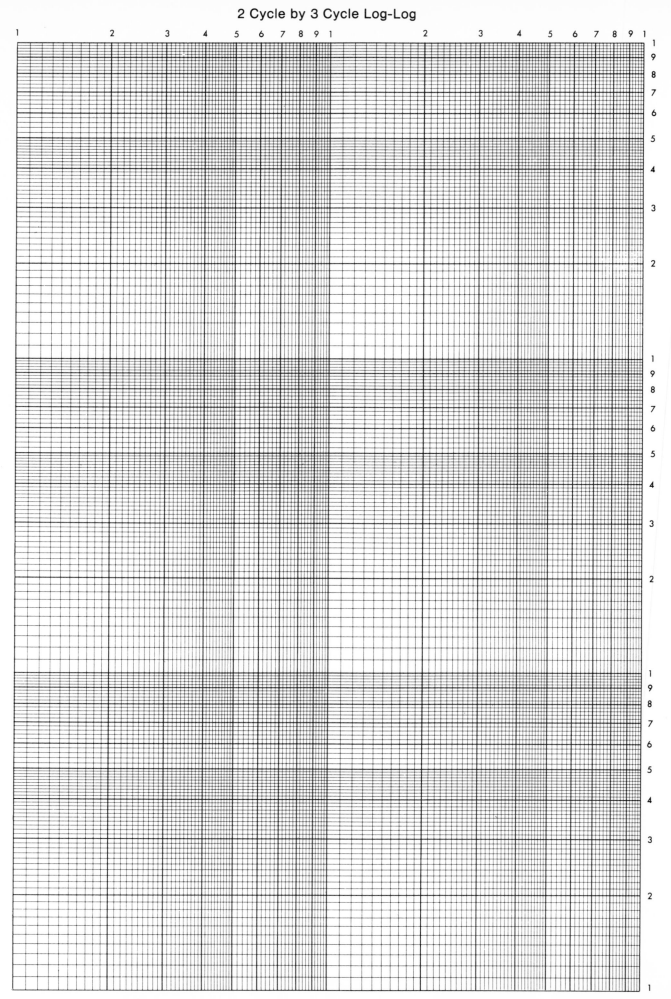

2 Cycle by 4 Cycle Log-Log

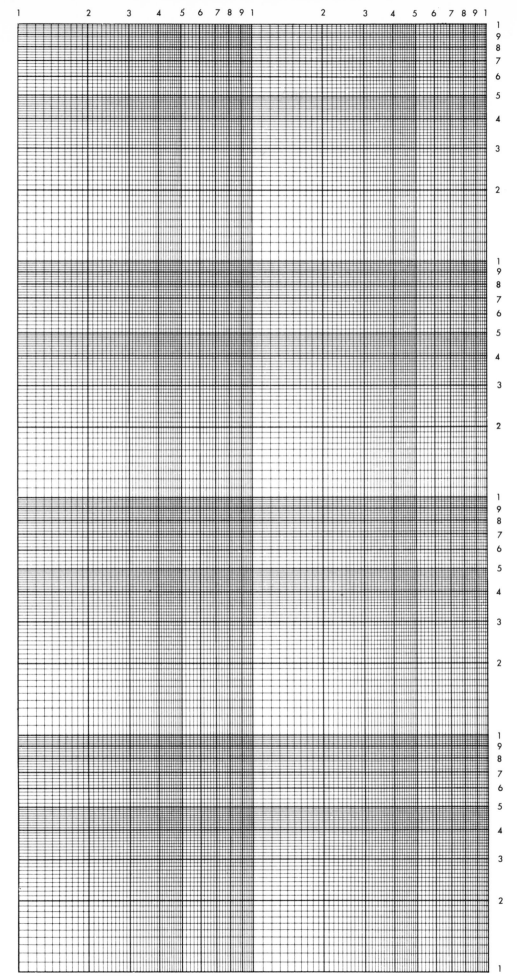

2 Cycle by 5 Cycle Log-Log

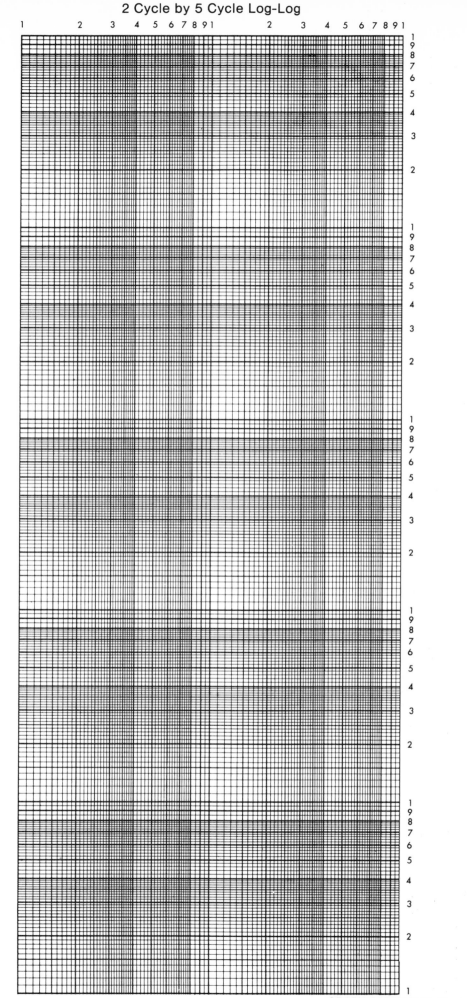

3 Cycle by 1 Cycle Log-Log

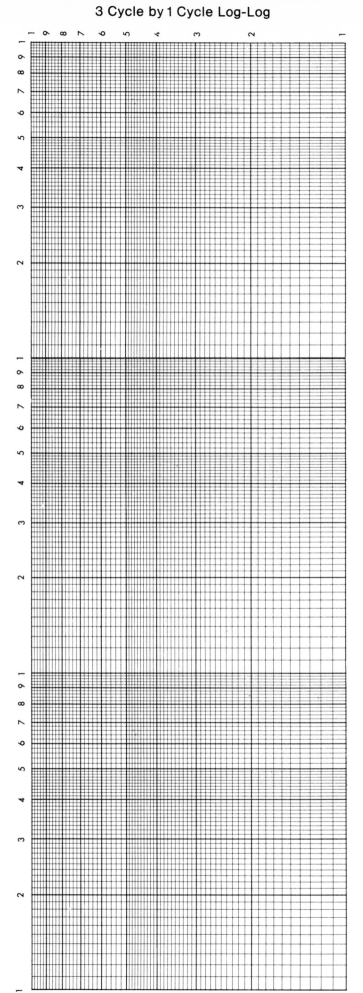

3 Cycle by 2 Cycle Log-Log

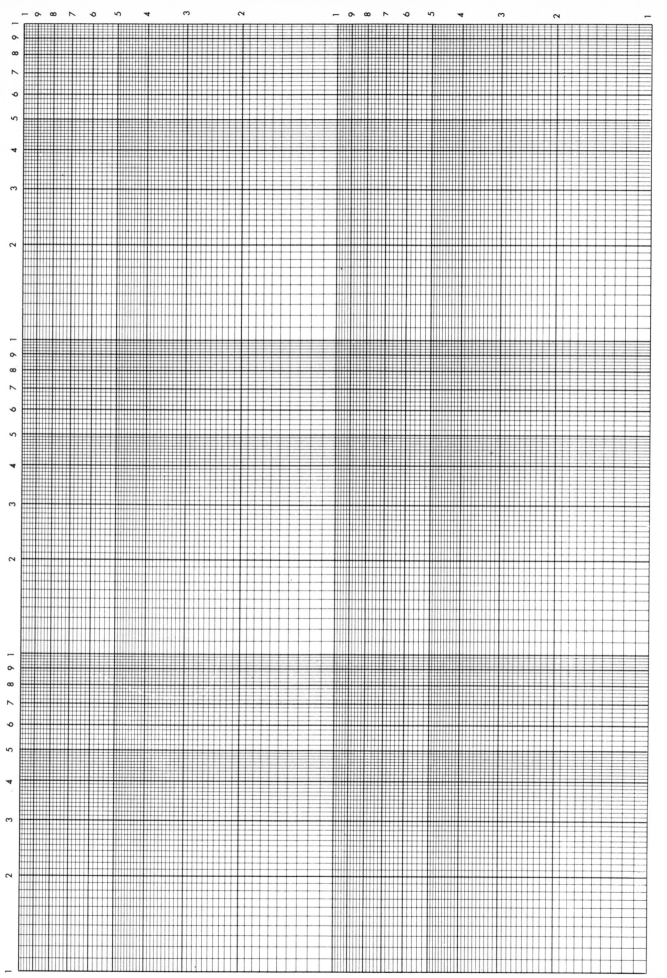

3 Cycle by 3 Cycle Log-Log

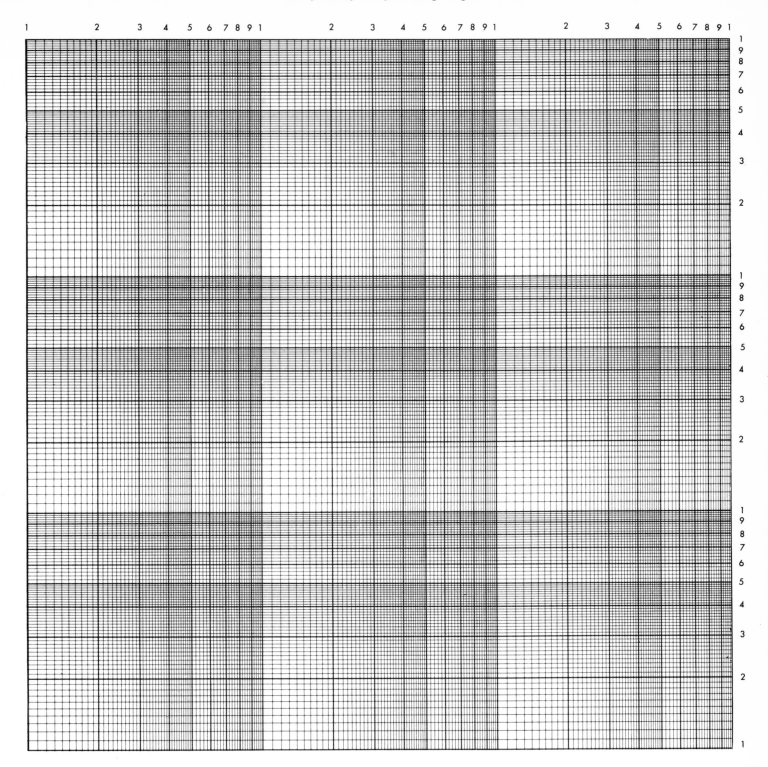

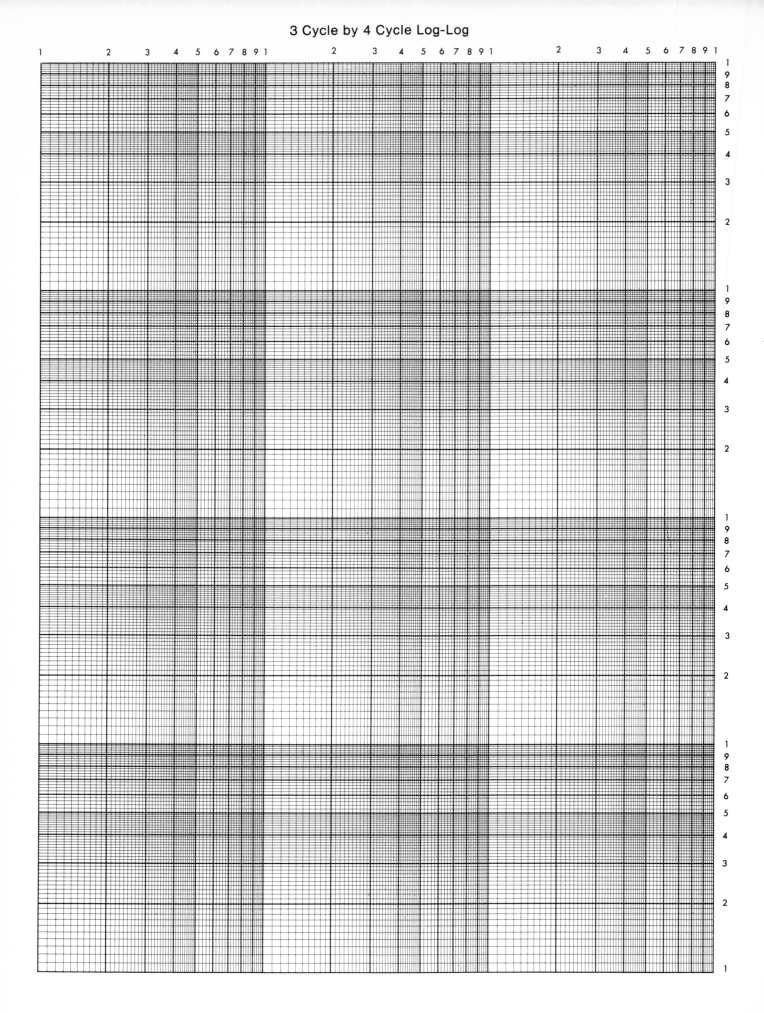

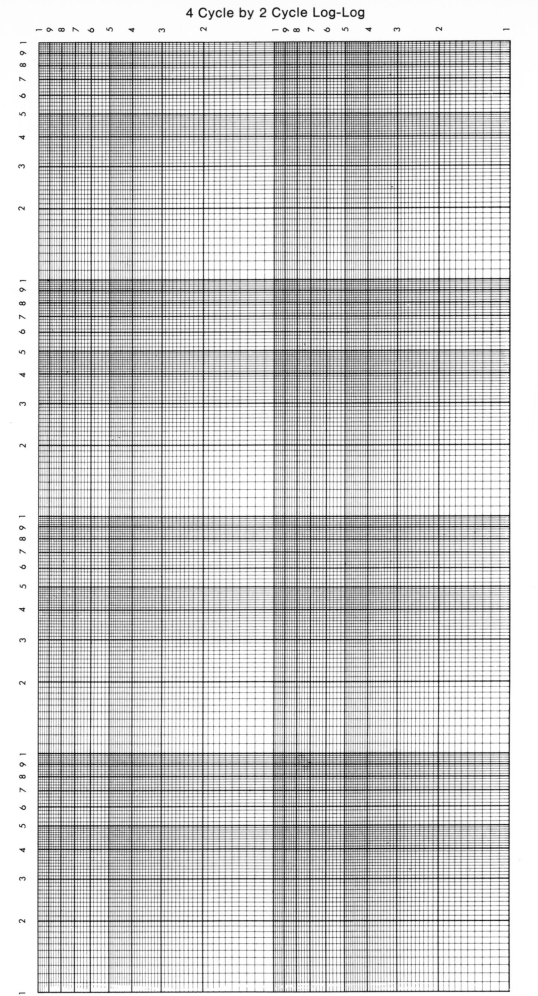

GRAPH PAPER From Your COPIER—**HPBooks**

4 Cycle by 3 Cycle Log-Log

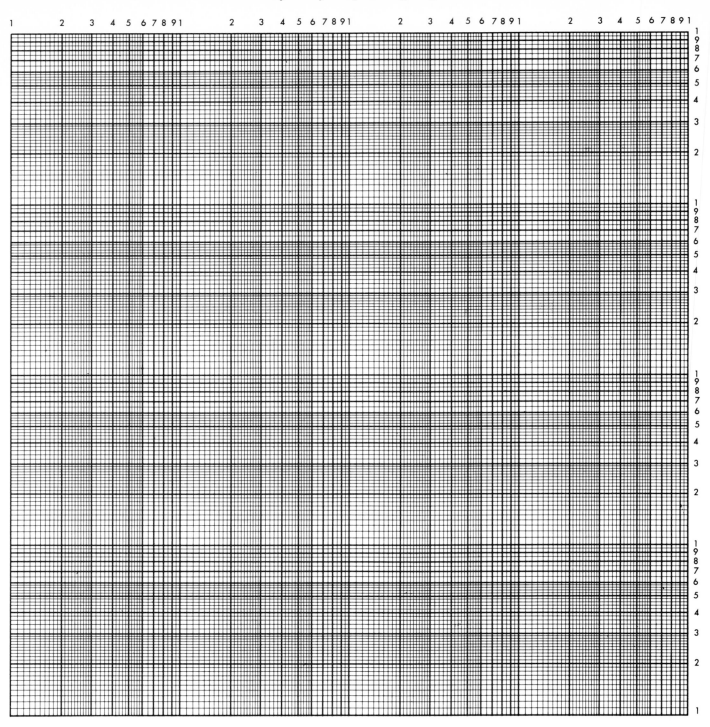

4 Cycle by 6 Cycle Log-Log

5 Cycle by 2 Cycle Log-Log

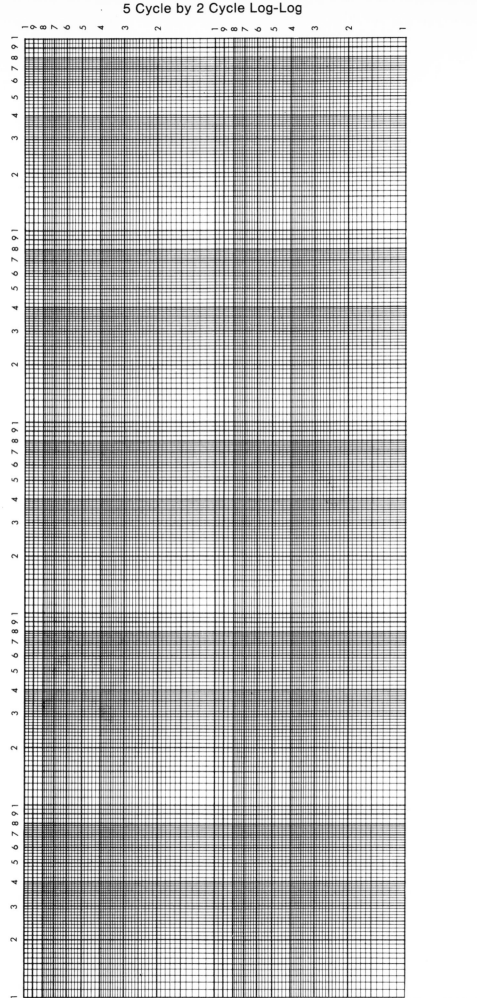

5 Cycle by 3 Cycle Log-Log

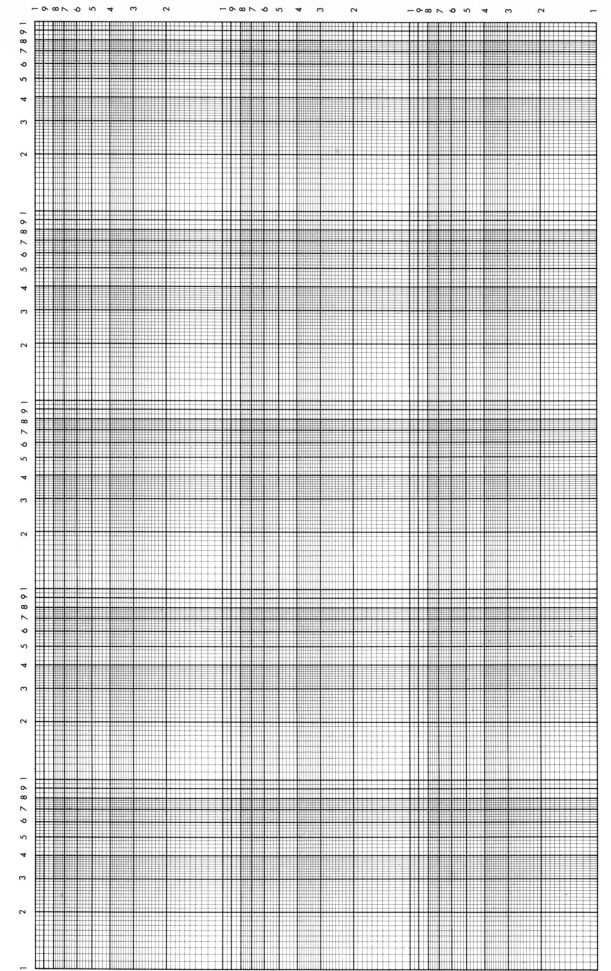

5 Cycle by 5 Cycle Log-Log

6 Cycle by 4 Cycle Log-Log

6 Cycle by 6 Cycle Log-Log

8 Cycle by 10 Cycle Log-Log

10 Cycle by 8 Cycle Log-Log

GRAPH PAPER From Your COPIER—**HPBooks**

GRAPH PAPER From Your COPIER—**HPBooks**

Perspective 12 x 12 x 8 box

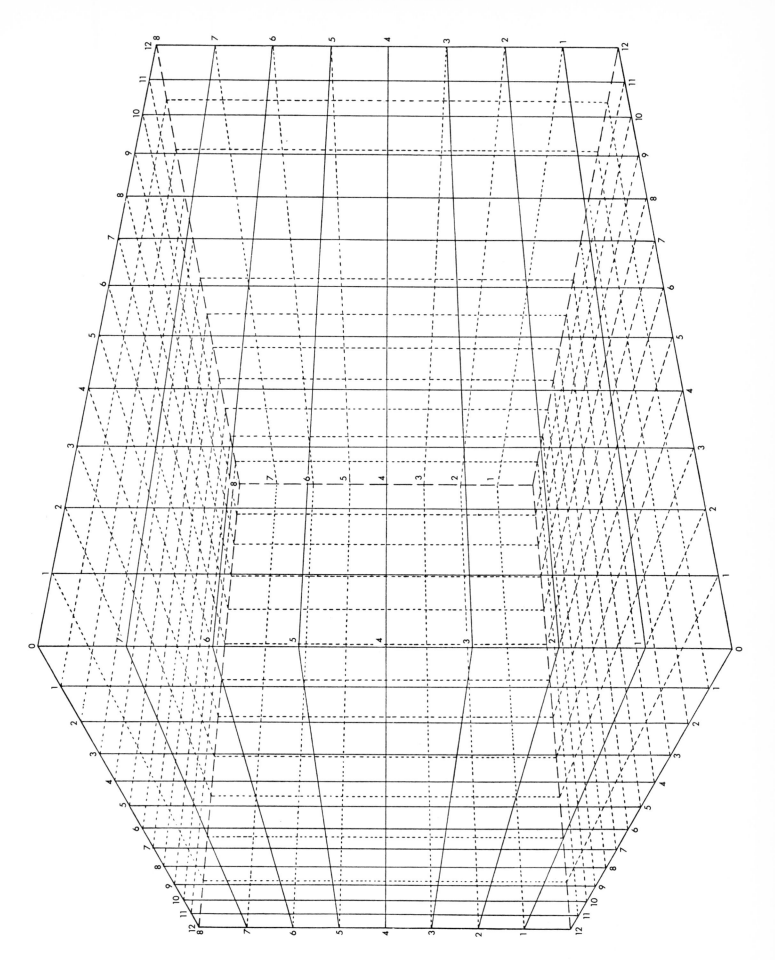

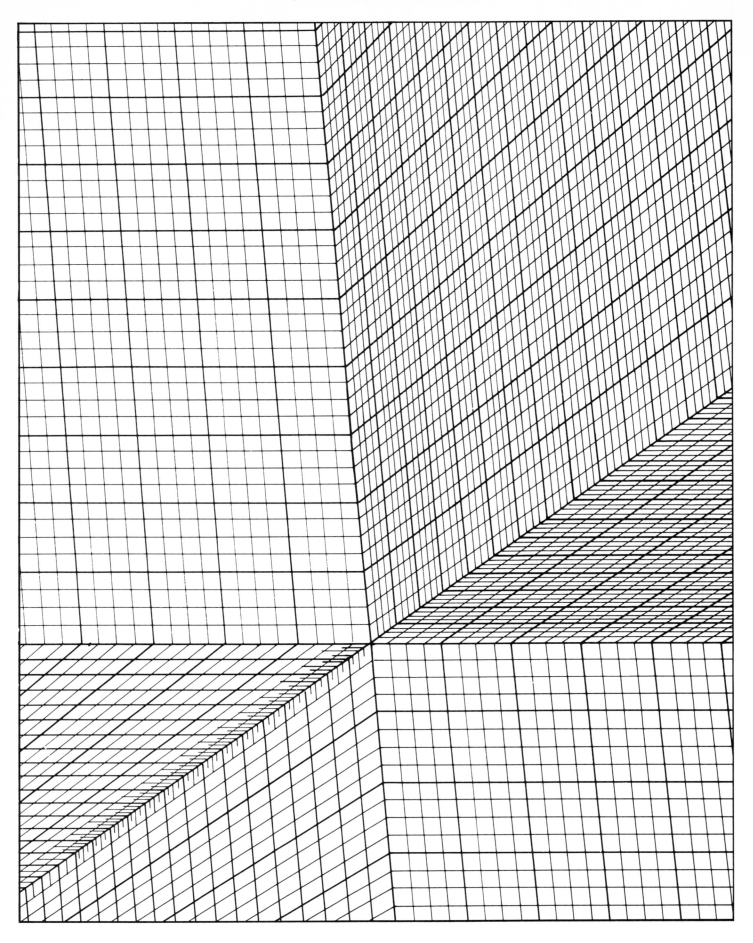

208

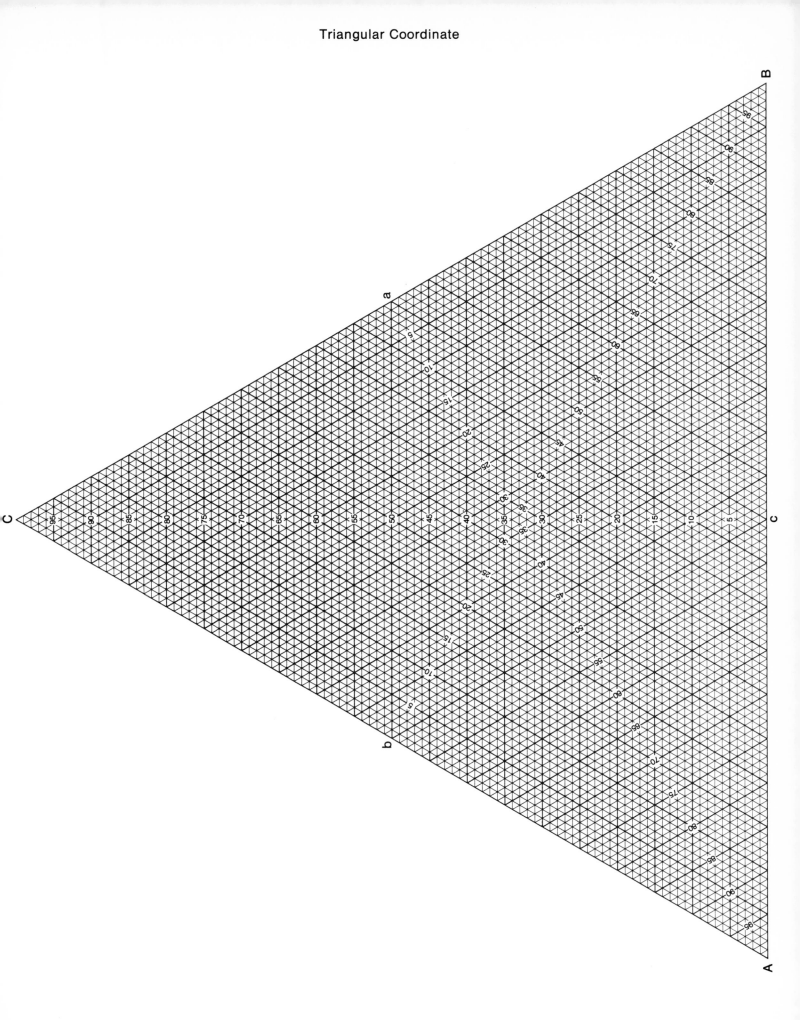

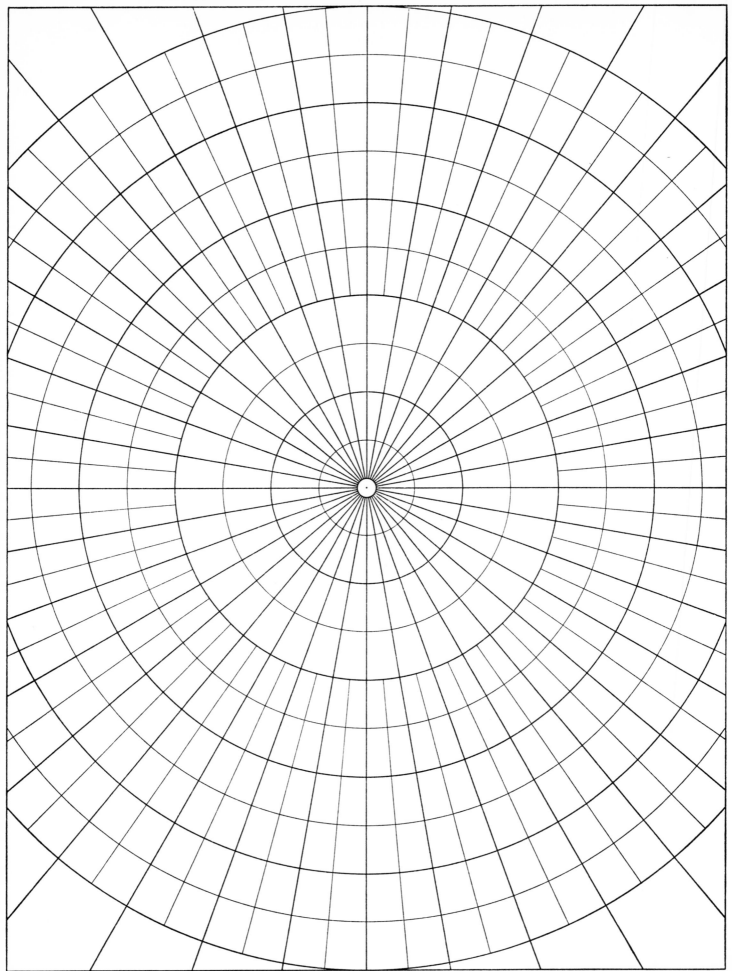

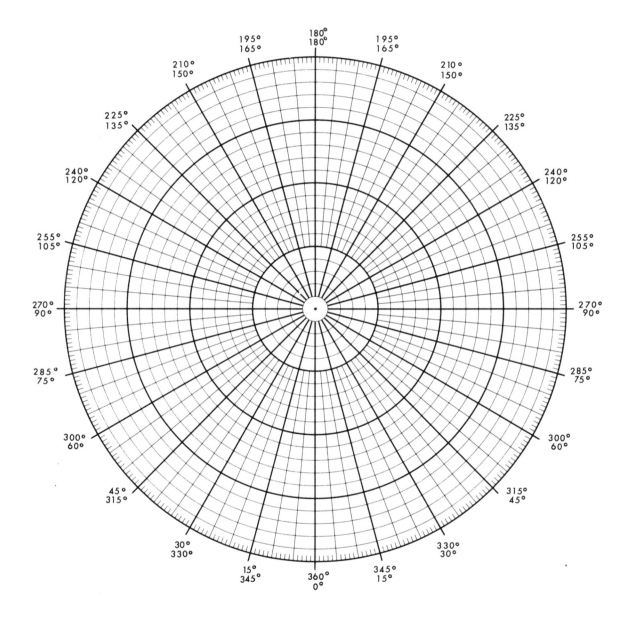

Polar Coordinate, Radius 50 Divisions 5th Accent, Circumference 1°, 10° Divisions

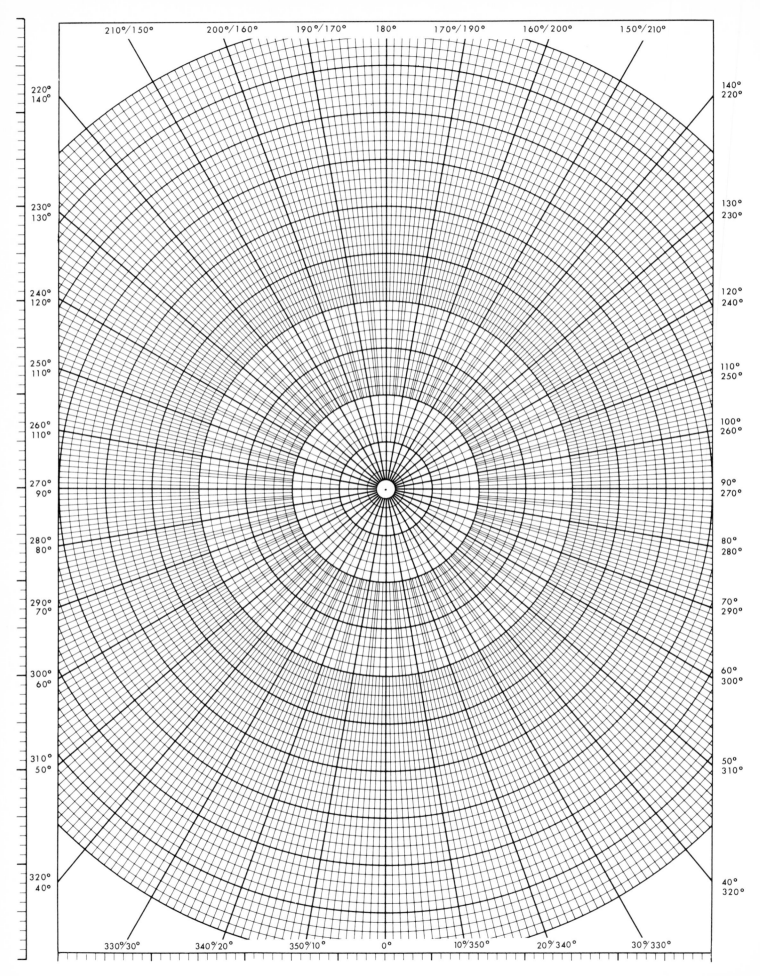

Polar Coordinate, Radius 55 Divisions 5th Accent, Circumference 2°, 10° Divisions

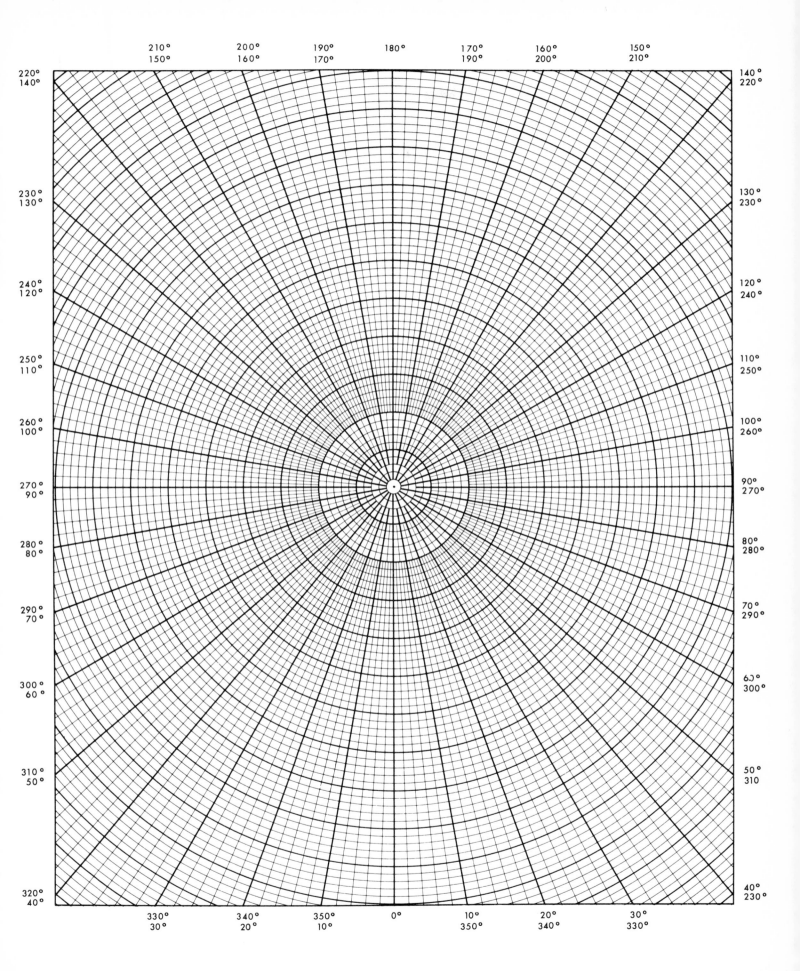

Polar Coordinate, Radius 70 Divisions 5th Accent, Circumference 2°, 10° Divisions

GRAPH PAPER From Your COPIER—**HPBooks**

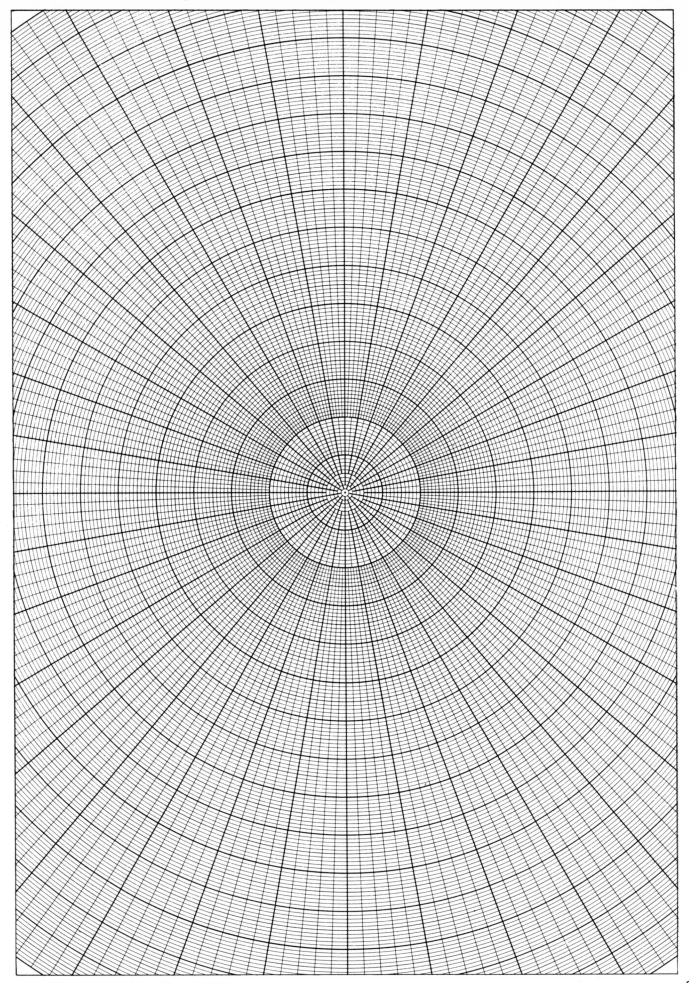

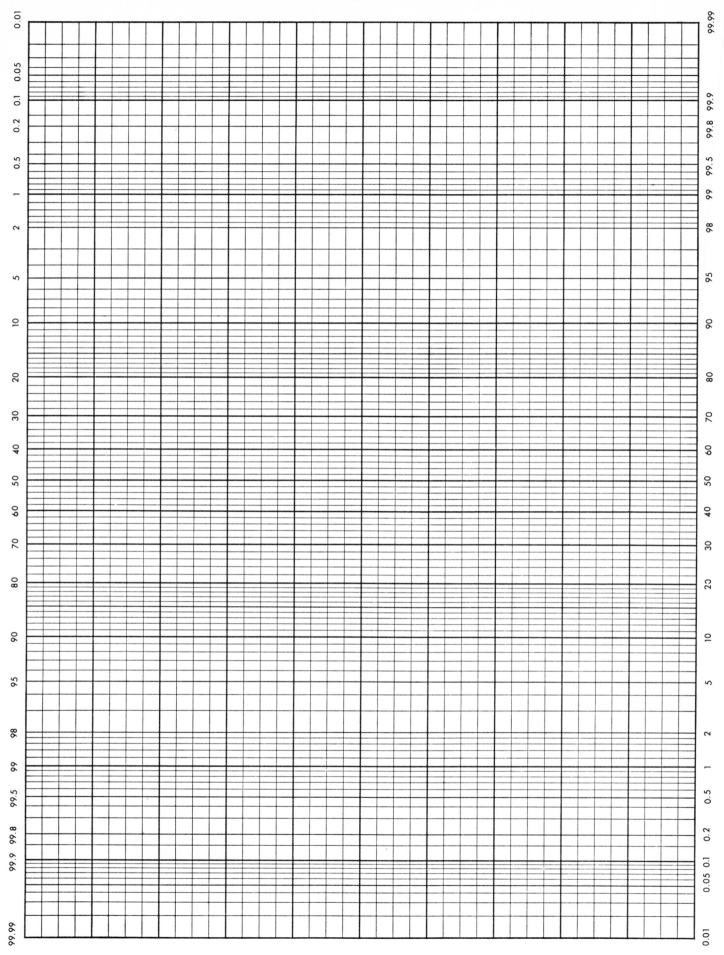

Probability by 80 Divisions

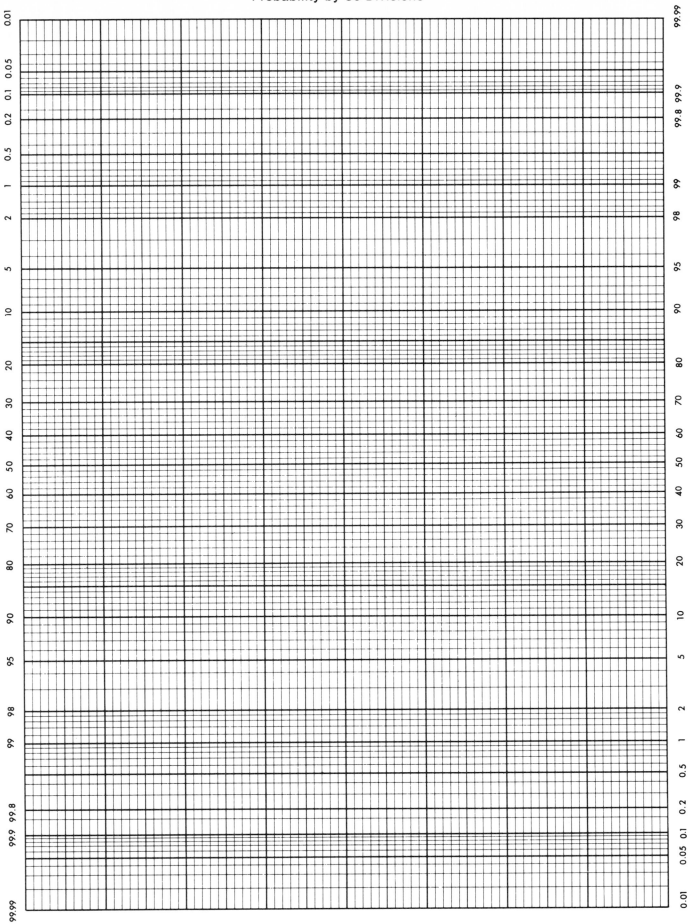

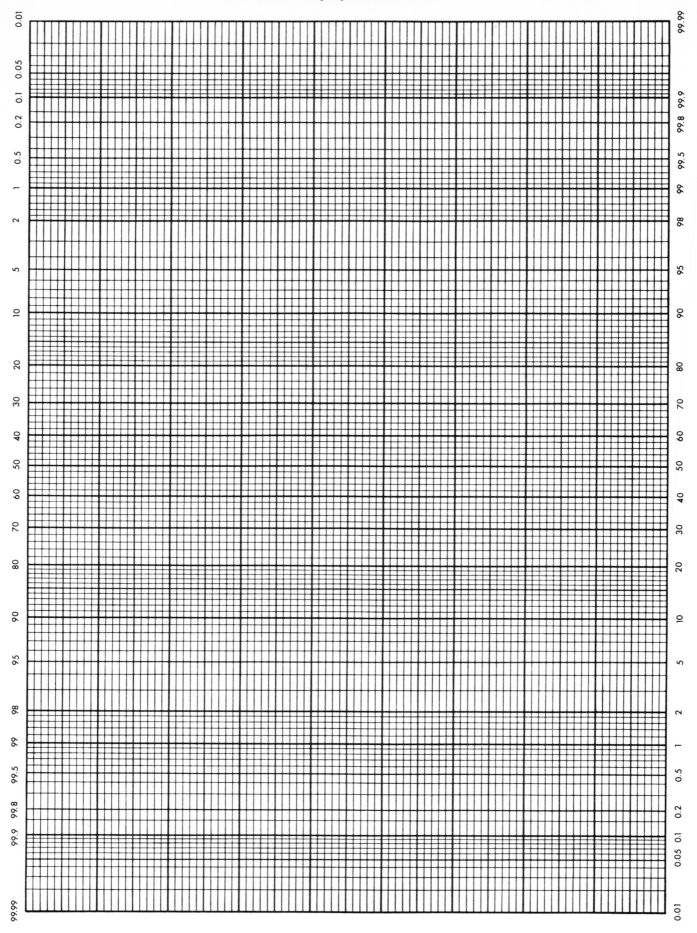

GRAPH PAPER From Your COPIER—**HPBooks**

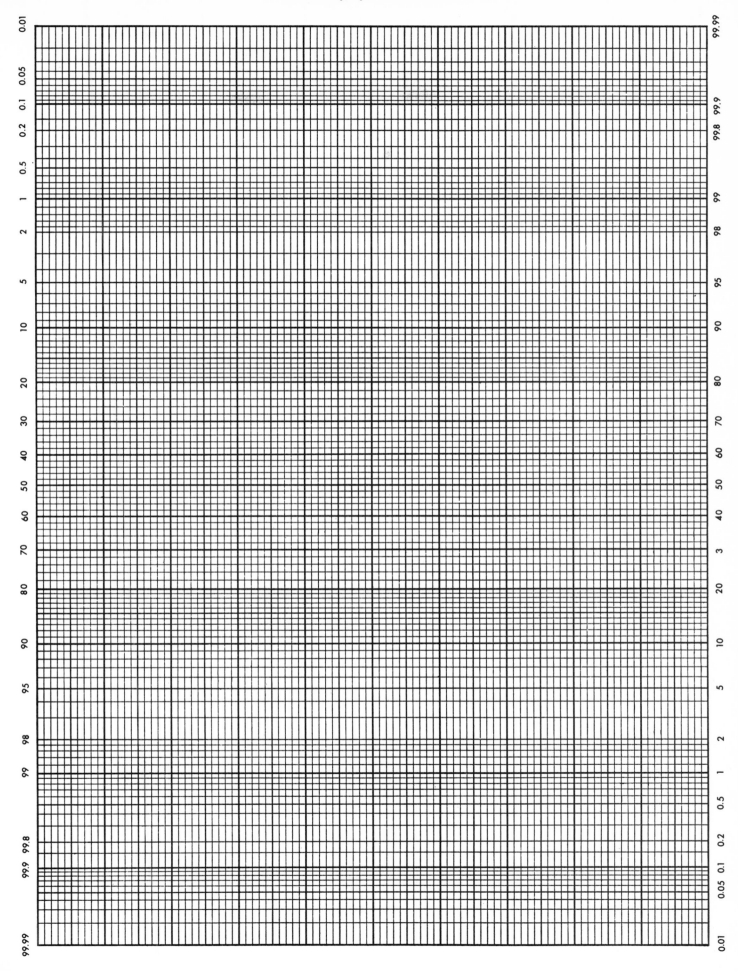

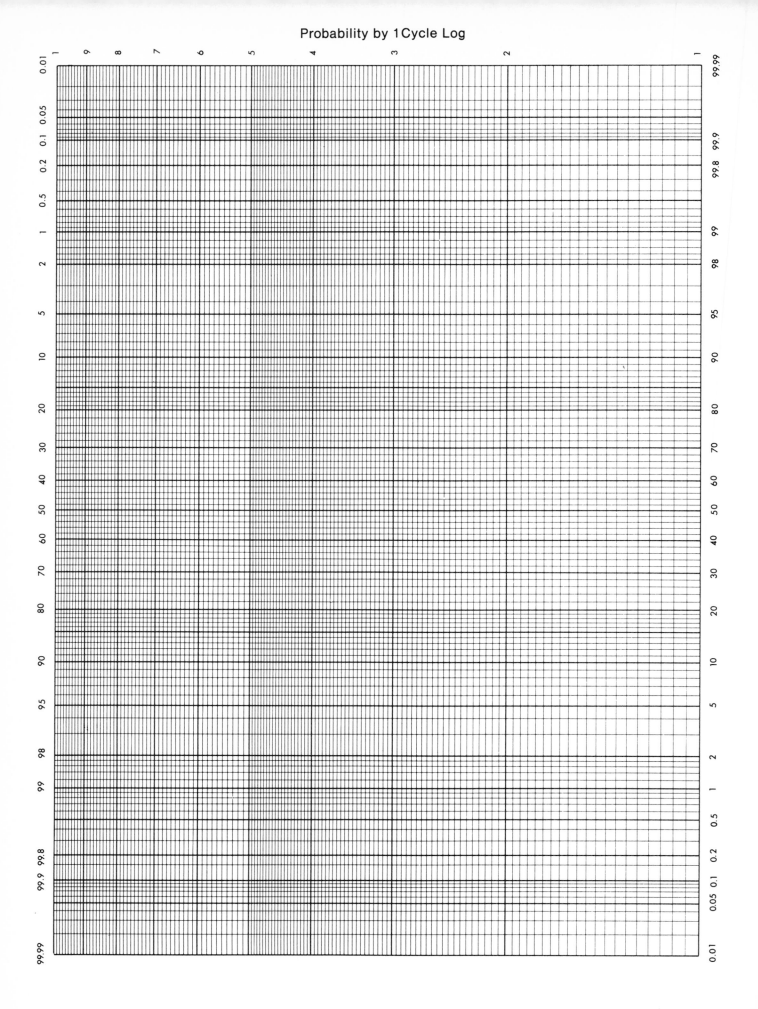

Probability by 2 Cycle Log

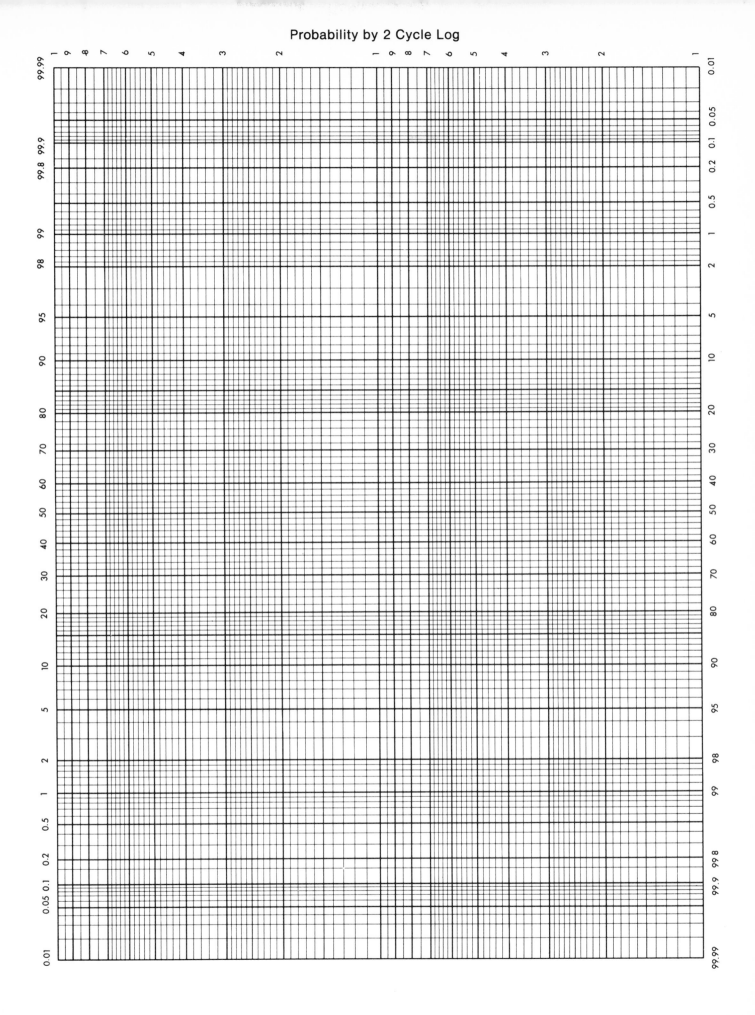

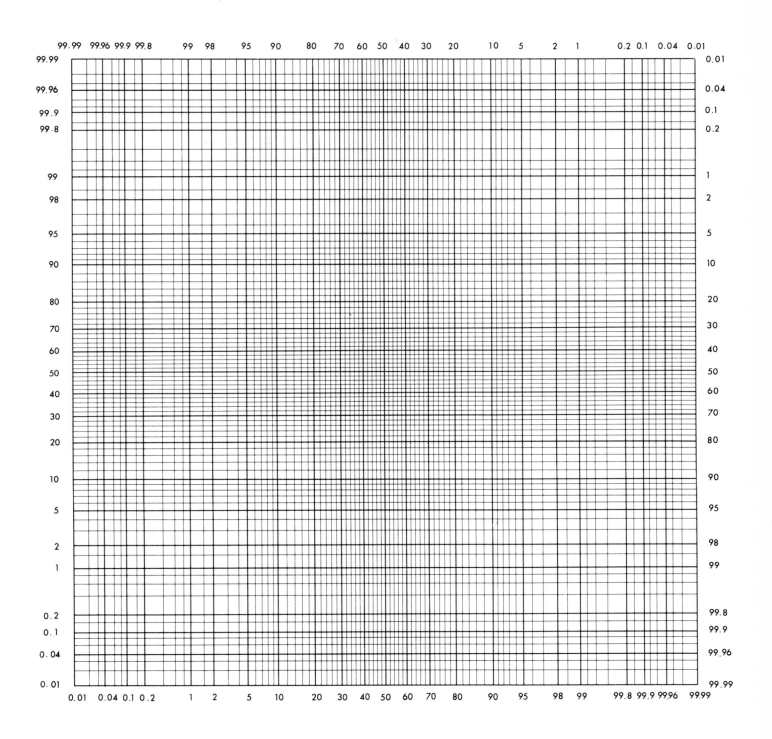

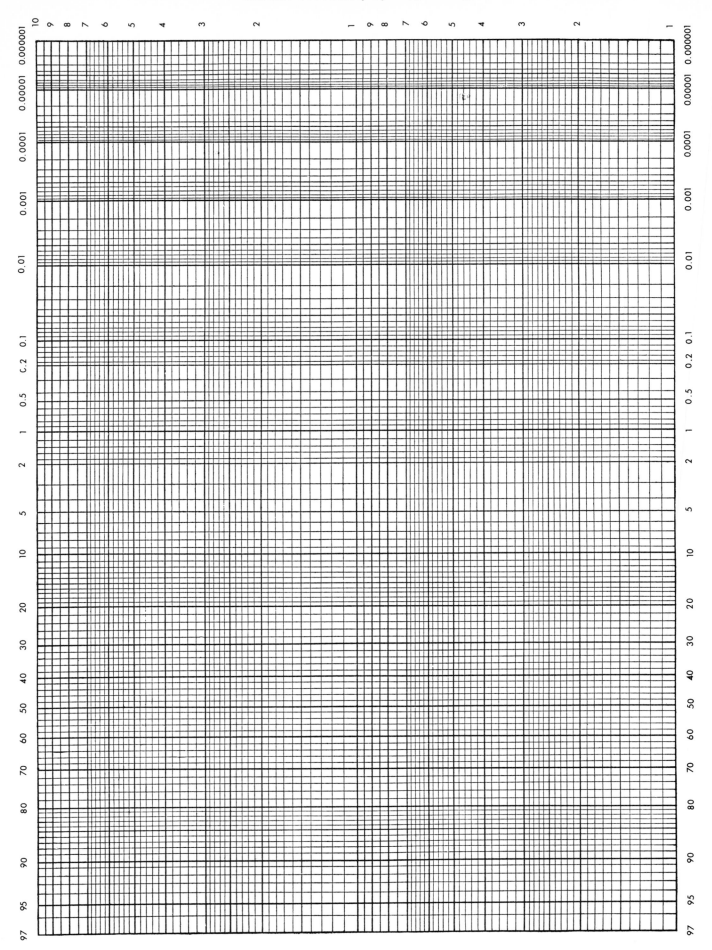

Probability by 3 Cycle Log with Probit Scale

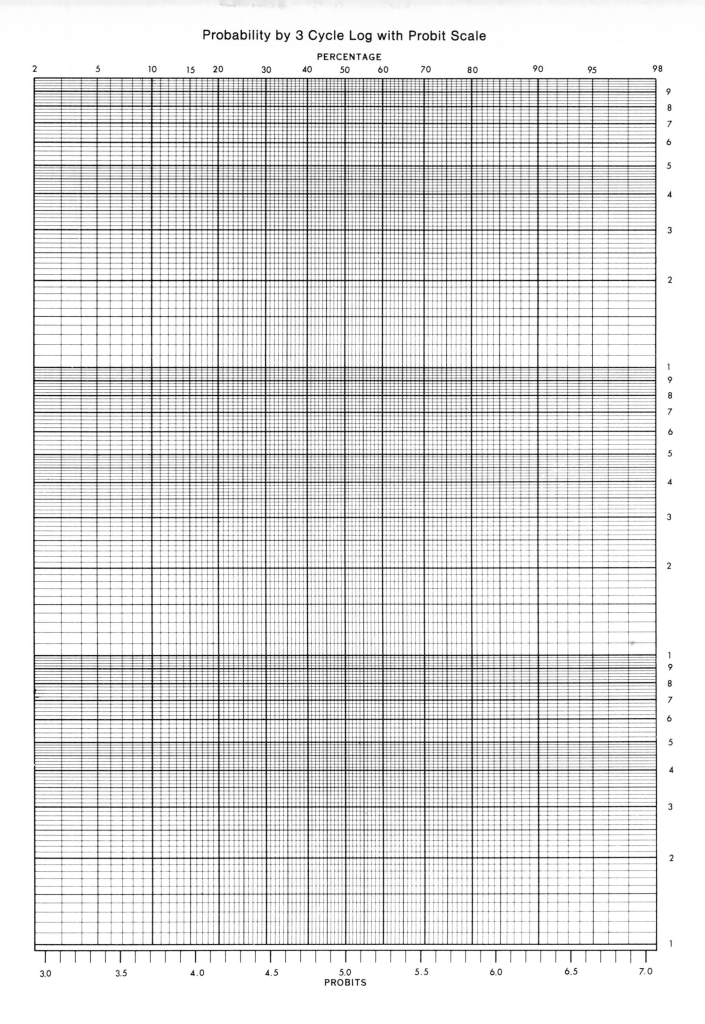

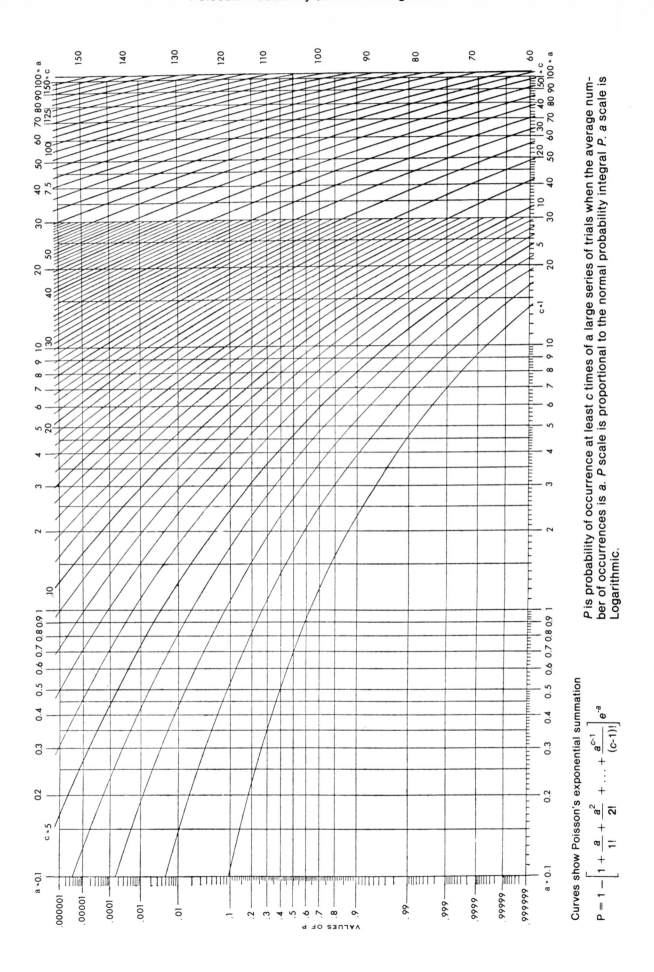

P is probability of occurrence at least *c* times of a large series of trials when the average number of occurrences is *a*. *P* scale is proportional to the normal probability integral *P*. *a* scale is Logarithmic.

Curves show Poisson's exponential summation

$$P = 1 - \left[1 + \frac{a}{1!} + \frac{a^2}{2!} + \dots + \frac{a^{c-1}}{(c-1)!}\right]e^{-a}$$

VALUES OF P

Permille Probability by 80 Divisions

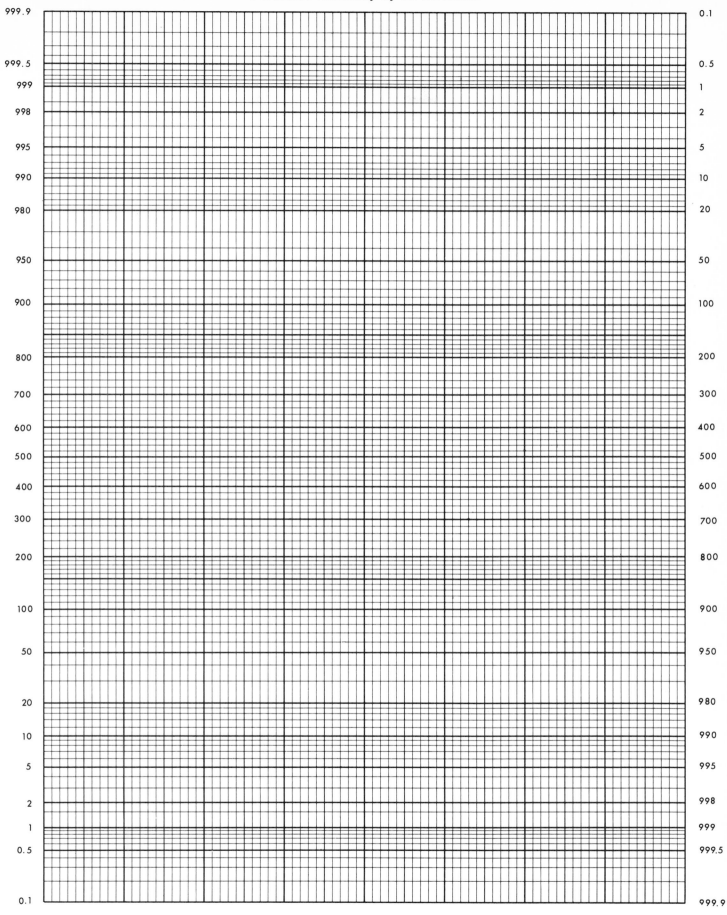

Weibull Probability by 2 Cycle Log

⊙ *Estimation Point*

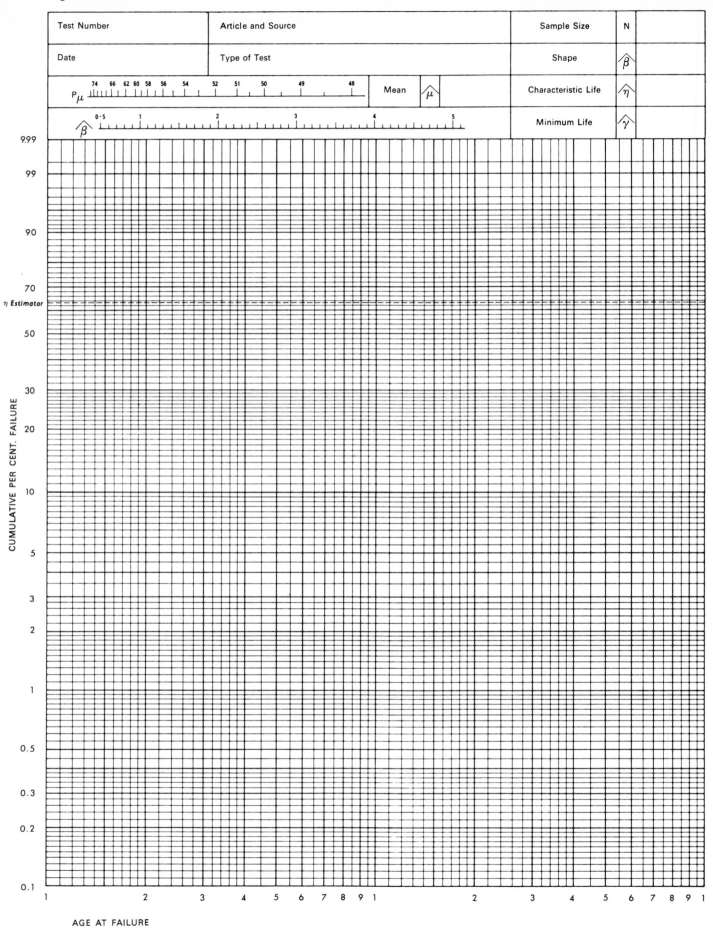

CUMULATIVE PER CENT. FAILURE

AGE AT FAILURE

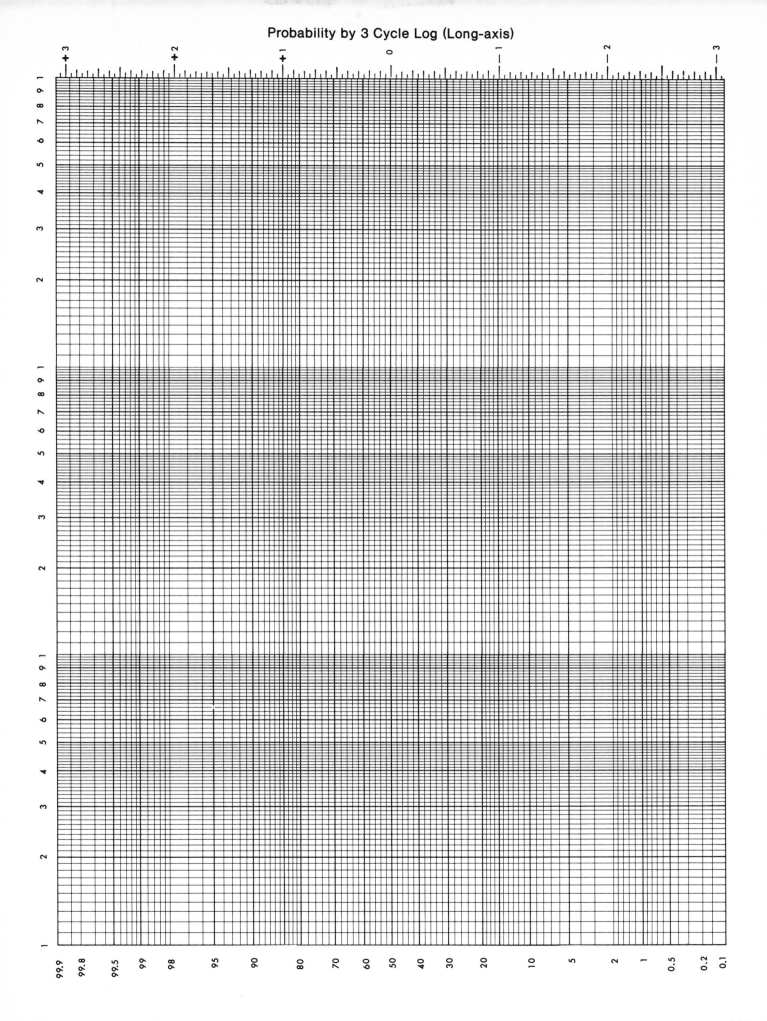

Extended Weibull Probability by 3 Cycle Log

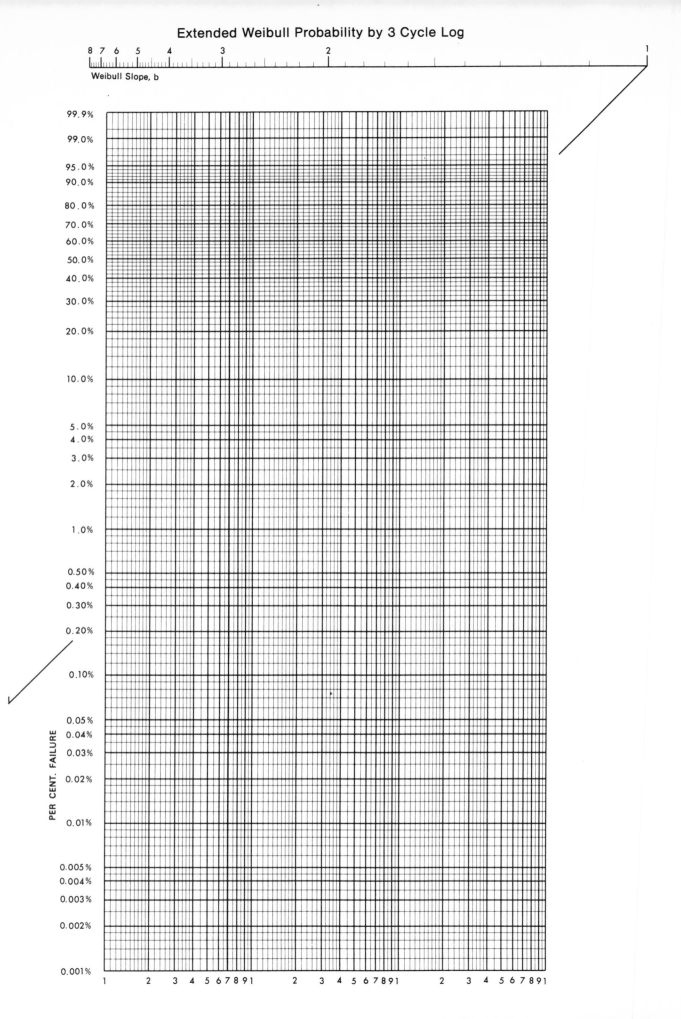

Poisson Probability (*a* scale is arithmetic 0 to 15 with 10 divisions per unit)

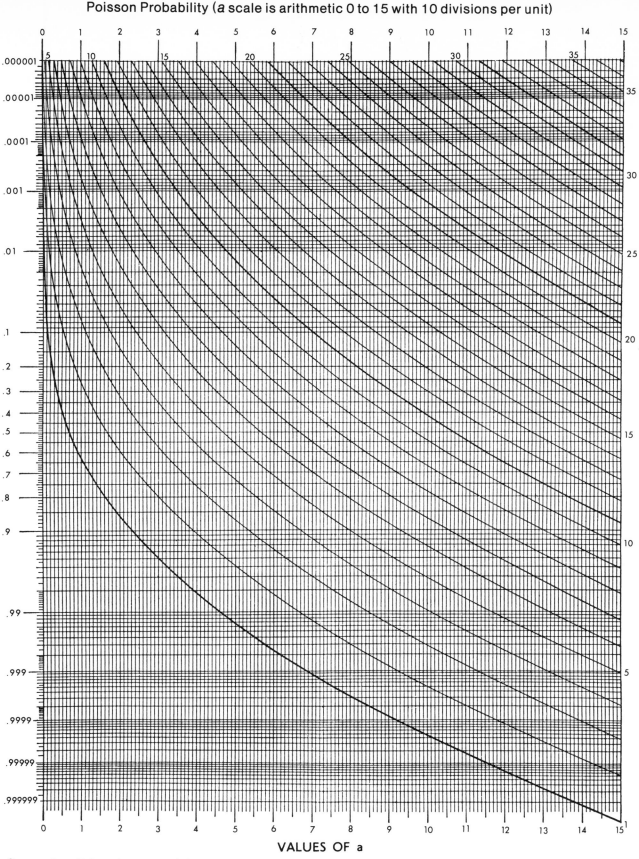

VALUES OF a

Curves show Poisson's exponential summation

$$P = 1 - \left[1 + \frac{a}{1!} + \frac{a^2}{2!} + \ldots + \frac{a^{c-1}}{(c-1)!}\right]e^{-a}$$

P is probability of occurrence at least *c* times of a large series of trials when the average number of occurrences is *a*. *P* scale is proportional to the normal probability integral *P*. *a* scale is Logarithmic.

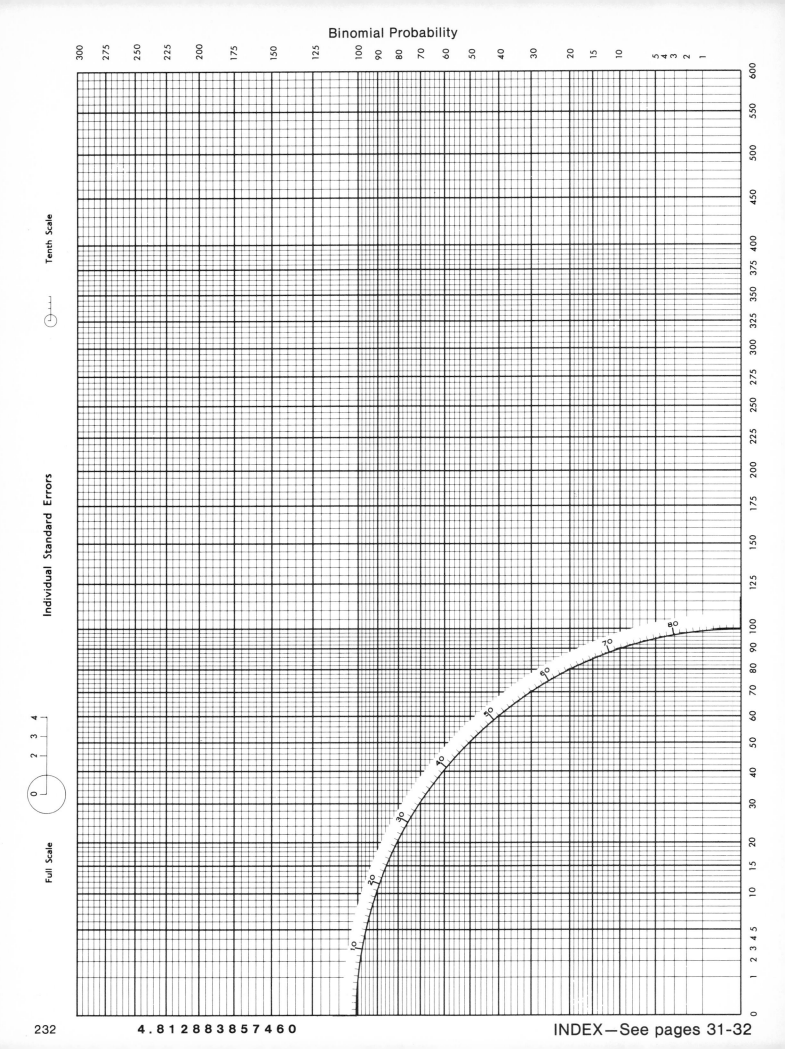

Binomial Probability

Individual Standard Errors

Tenth Scale

Full Scale

4.812883857460

INDEX—See pages 31-32

ORDER MORE COPIES—FOR YOURSELF OR FRIENDS!

GRAPH PAPER FROM YOUR COPIER

To order this sensational new book, simply complete the information below. Send check or money order only. Allow 3 to 4 weeks delivery by mail.

_____ copy(ies) of GRAPH PAPER FROM YOUR COPIER at $12.95 each. $ _____

Add 75¢ postage and handling for each book. _____

Arizona residents add 6% sales tax (78¢ per book). _____

TOTAL ENCLOSED $ _____

NAME _____

ADDRESS _____

CITY/STATE/ZIP _____

Mail to:

HPBooks Box 5367, Dept. GC-50, Tucson, AZ 85703

GRAPH PAPER FROM YOUR COPIER

To order this sensational new book, simply complete the information below. Send check or money order only. Allow 3 to 4 weeks delivery by mail.

_____ copy(ies) of GRAPH PAPER FROM YOUR COPIER at $12.95 each. $ _____

Add 75¢ postage and handling for each book. _____

Arizona residents add 6% sales tax (78¢ per book). _____

TOTAL ENCLOSED $ _____

NAME _____

ADDRESS _____

CITY/STATE/ZIP _____

Mail to:

HPBooks Box 5367, Dept. GC-50, Tucson, AZ 85703

GRAPH PAPER FROM YOUR COPIER

To order this sensational new book, simply complete the information below. Send check or money order only. Allow 3 to 4 weeks delivery by mail.

_____ copy(ies) of GRAPH PAPER FROM YOUR COPIER at $12.95 each. $ _____

Add 75¢ postage and handling for each book. _____

Arizona residents add 6% sales tax (78¢ per book). _____

TOTAL ENCLOSED $ _____

NAME _____

ADDRESS _____

CITY/STATE/ZIP _____

Mail to:

HPBooks Box 5367, Dept. GC-50, Tucson, AZ 85703

GRAPH PAPER FROM YOUR COPIER

To order this sensational new book, simply complete the information below. Send check or money order only. Allow 3 to 4 weeks delivery by mail.

_____ copy(ies) of GRAPH PAPER FROM YOUR COPIER at $12.95 each. $ _____

Add 75¢ postage and handling for each book. _____

Arizona residents add 6% sales tax (78¢ per book). _____

TOTAL ENCLOSED $ _____

NAME _____

ADDRESS _____

CITY/STATE/ZIP _____

Mail to:

HPBooks Box 5367, Dept. GC-50, Tucson, AZ 85703